E

"When I read, "Prayer, The Power Beyond," I was delighted to be privileged to read such a magnificent book, overflowing with the handiwork inspired by God almighty. This enormous book is the most compelling devotional book, I've read to date, it is fresh breathed, laced with The Holy Spirit and the uniqueness of a writer in the background, once silenced, hidden, now delighted to bring forth his treasure. Others know these are down loads from the throne room of God and are priceless, heartfelt encounters with Father God to inspire you on reckless days; when you can only hear and feel your own heart. This book is directed to give you a road to travel and a sky with a horizon that never ends.

Susan Sengezer: best-selling author, Minister, RN, Radio Host "The Advocate"

Charles Johnson is one of the most giving and gracious men I know. Charles and I met about seven years ago in a Saturday morning men's Bible study. When you spend time together studying the Word of God, sharing our hurts and pains and praying for one another, you really get to know a person. Charles is the real, authentic, caring man with insights for us to learn, especially when it comes to prayer. Charles' love for people is expressed in many ways, from the warm smile and words of encouragement he gives to everyone he meets, to the genuine desire to help people with their personal needs, especially by praying for them.

Charles' new book, *Prayer: The Power Beyond Belief*, is not just another book on prayer, but a book that builds up one's faith in an awesome God who desires everyone to seek Him in communicating, quietness, listening, confessing and declaring. He is truly an intercessor and a man of prayer. As a pastor and theologian, I highly recommend this thought-provoking, faith-giving book to you. As a friend, I highly recommend this life-changing book to you, because Charles knows the God of the "Power beyond Belief" and desires you to know Him too!

Rev. Daniel B. Gilbert, Ph.D.

Pastor of St. Stephen Presbyterian Church

President of EmPowered Living Int'l Ministries

Dear Charles,

I've spent a little time this weekend enjoying your book and am glad to endorse it. Thank you for sharing it with me. Anyone who reads these pages will benefit from a wealth of prayers, stories, encouragement, and wisdom. They are authentic and personal and reflect you and God's grace in you. Most of all, the readers will find themselves in fresh conversation with the living God and eager to live the new possibilities of life in Jesus Christ.

Warmly, George

George Hinman,

Senior Pastor University

Presbyterian Church, Seattle, Washington

Drawn from the experiences of the author, a man of deep integrity who follows passionately after Jesus, the book offers significant insights into the deep and dark longings and affections of the human heart, and the remedy that is found only through authentic, passionate prayer. The book offers intensely practical examples of prayer drawn from both scripture and the author's own intimate life spent on his knees in sincere supplication. It is thus a unique and significant reference for those who have longings too deep for words, needing practical prayer templates topically arranged. The book offers stories of miraculous renewal of lives significantly broken- renewal that defies mere human explanation, renewal only found by the merciful, gracious hand of the Savior.

Blessings,

Roger A. Dermody

Deputy Executive Director for Missions

Presbyterian Mission Agency

Presbyterian Church (USA)

I read Charles Johnson's manuscript, and I can tell you it was a delightful, inspirational read.

Not only did I find Prayer....The Power Beyond Belief to be Christian based, but faith based, speaking to that part of us which is searching for the pathway to a more purpose driven, positive way of life.

Charles calls it a "feel good book" and I agree.

Mark A. Brewer

Former Senior Pastor, Bel Air Presbyterian Church

"This book speaks from the heart of a man who has experienced the sweet communion that can come only from meaningful and purposeful time spent in prayer with our loving Father in heaven. Charles Johnson's gift to us is his God given ability to thoughtfully articulate the intimacy that he enjoys with the Lord in such a way that the reader is truly inspired to delve deeper into their own personal prayer life.

Mark Wracher

Former County Director

Fellowship of Christian Athletes in Los Angeles (May 19, 2004)

Former Team Chaplain

Los Angeles Kings hockey club

PRAYER, THE POWER BEYOND

BELIEF

The greatest sin loose in the world today, is the sin of prayerlessness.

PRAYER, THE POWER
BEYOND BELIEF

BY

CHARLES JOHNSON

CONTENTS

ABOUT THIS BOOK 17

AUTHOR'S NOTE 19

ACKNOWLEDGMENTS 21

DEDICATION..25

FORWARD 27

SECTION ONE 31

REALITY CHECK..33

GUARD YOUR THOUGHTS 35

FOR A LONG AND HEALTHY LIFE..............39

"Prayers of Light"..39

"Wholeness of Life" 39

"Upon Awakening" 39

"Dealing With People" 40

"That Quiet Voice" 40

"Accepting God's Gift" 40

"Stand Strong" 41

"With Clasped Hands, Release the Holy Spirit Within" ...42

"Move With Authority" 43

"Give with a Healthy Heart"...............................45

"Take a Mental Shower" 45

"Resolve" 47

"First Light" 47

"Driving To Work" 48

"Divine Encounters" 48

"A Moveable Feast" 49

"Grip of Steel" 49

"Advocates for Women's Rights" 49

"Thy Will Be Done" 50

"Friendship" 51

"High Tea With God" 51

"Heartfelt" 52

"Soul Healing" 52

"Wonder of Wonders" 53

"Shared Yoke" 53

"Church Of Choice" 55

SECTION TWO 57

A JOYFUL NEW YOU 59

USE THE POWER AND AUTHORITY OF THE
SPOKEN WORD...61

THREE KEYS TO SUCCESS 63

MIRACULOUS STORIES OF FAITH.................................69

"God and the Butterfly"......................................69

"Not Just Coincidence".....................................74

"A Life Yet To Live"..75

"Who Does Your Hate Hurt"............................77

"The Called Minister".......................................82

"Book Of Records"..95

"Angel & the Baby"...98

"The Power of Prayer".....................................101

"No Greater Gift Than Love" 104

"False Voice"..110

SELECTED BIBLE VERSES AND THOUGHTS TO
STRENGTHEN WHEN IN NEED 117

SECTION THREE...129

FROM THE HEART...131

THOUGHTS AND ACTIVITIES THAT HELPED ME
OVERCOME..133

"Rise With Joy" 133

"The Dark of Night" 133

"Winter Love" 135

"Reaching For Freedom"..................................142

"Put Reality on Hold".......................................142

"Dance Away Your Cares"................................143

"Reflections"..143

"Touched By Hidden Feelings".........................144

"Reconstructing"...145

"Fear and Doubts" 146

"The True You" 148

"The Living God" 150

"Take the Time" 151

CELEBRATE LIFE BY SHARING THE BLESSING...153

"The Joy Around Us" 153

"Rich man/Poor man/Beggar man" 153

"Open the Windows of Your Heart" 154

"Extend a Helping Hand" 154

"With A Warm Loving Heart" 155

"Sharing the Gift"..155

"Reaffirming the Joys of Love".......................156

"The Beauty Within" 157

"Elegant Ebony Woman" 157

"Be Not the Bearer of Grudges" 158

"Fifty/Sixty/Seventy Years And Still Going"...................158

"Being There" 159

"Alone, But Not Lonely"..................................159

"Minister to the Needy" 160

"A Prayer of Thanksgiving" 161

"Where the Heart Is" 161

"Celebrate Life by Giving" 162

"True Joy Is Sharing" 162

"Clown for a Day" 162

"Unfulfilled Dreams" 163

"Now I Lay Me Down To Sleep" 163

"Another Day" 164

SECTION FOUR 165

PERSONAL AND WORLD PRAYERS FOR
INDIVIDUALS AND UNIVERSAL HEALING 167

"Abandonment" 167

"Vision Prayer, For a Lost Sheep" 167

"Alcoholism and Substance Abuse" 168

"Anger" 169

"Betrayal" 169

"Choices" 170

"Disabled" 170

"Empty the Vessel" 172

"Fear of Success" 172

"Financial Loss" 173

"Freedom to Succeed" 173

"Grief" 175

"Harmony"...176

"He Heals Me From Within" 177

"Infertile" 177

"Infertility" 177

"Isolation"..178

"Issues of Health" 178

"Love's Power" 179

"Making a Living"...179

"Need of Employment" 180

"Not a Burden, But a Joy" 180

"Partner of My Own"..181

"Self-pity"..181

"Universal Healing Prayer, Time for Healing" 182

"Wisdom" 183

"Unification of Churches" 184

IN PARTING...185

ABOUT THE AUTHOR 187

ABOUT THIS BOOK

Prayer, The Power Beyond Belief, is a book written to inspire and uplift the human spirit, of all people: Christians, non-Christian, young and old and those in-between.

It is a source book, something a reader may carry into everyday life and refer to, to bring a smile on a not so great day, or uplift a heavy heart, in times of stress. Or, it may be used as a Clarion call to remind us of the beauty of life; within and without.

And, at all times, this book reminds us that the glass may be viewed as half full or half empty; depending on the way we perceive the grandeur of the universe, the wonders of the soul, and the precious breath of life; which energizes us from the beginning of life, to the end.

In short, it is a highly charged battery cable for the soul, designed to jump start, the reader's faith, in the power -- beyond belief.

AUTHOR'S NOTE

This manuscript came into being much like pearls come into being, but instead of being in a shell with sand scraping my brain, my thoughts were continually irritated by the statement, "Prayer is the greatest weapon" that the Christian has in their fight against the forces of darkness. For our struggle is not against flesh and blood, but against the world forces of this darkness, against the spiritual forces of wickedness in the heavenly places.

As I thought more about this, it dawned upon me that a weapon is something used in a fight or a battle. But, Jesus defeated our enemy, and the victory is ours. So, I reasoned, that prayer is the greatest tool that the Christian has as they/we journey through life.

Prayer is the key to finding the answers to life's issues, for prayer is conversation with God, and the Holy Spirit, the helper Jesus graced us with, so that we would not be left alone, afraid and adrift on the stormy seas of life.

With the gift of prayer and the indwelling Holy Spirit, we can sleep peacefully in the boat, as God guides us through the roughest times.

So, I urge you, brothers and sisters, pray often and without ceasing, and remember." I can do more than pray after I have prayed, but I really cannot do more than pray, until I have prayed.

ACKNOWLEDGMENTS

I give thanks and gratitude to my mother, Bessie June Johnson, who brought me to faith while I was nursing mother's milk.

I give thanks and gratitude to my eldest sister who has fed me a diet of "Be loving and life will love you back," for as long as I can remember. And, to this day, she remains a positive force in my life.

I give thanks and gratitude to my dear departed sister who shared her passion for books and literature with me, and inspired me to write. And, I give thanks to my son and his wife. They restore my faith in the institution of marriage, by the way they nurture and support each other, through rough and smooth times, and like the potter with clay, they form each other's character, making each other a better person; always using TLC, with a dash of tough LOVE!

I am deeply grateful to my older brother and my niece who are sitting at that big banquet table in the sky, with my mother and father who stood up for me, when it really counted. I thank them for helping me become the being I am today, a child of the most High God, and a faithful servant of my Lord and Savior Jesus Christ.

And, I am deeply indebted to the following people:

Mr. Jack and Jean Pegram, they helped me up when I was down.

Dr. Michael Lehmann Boddicker and Mrs. Edie Lehmann Boddicker, for opening their home for a 10 year Bible study, where we perused the Bible from cover to cover.

Rev. Kim Dorr Tilley of the Beacon and entertainment ministry department for a tireless devotion to helping people in the motion picture industry navigate the stormy world of show business, and keep a moral compass in the face of many levels of perilous temptation; by always offering Godly Counsel.

Mrs. Ellen Baker, Clerk of Session and Children's Discipleship Coordinator for Bel Air Presbyterian Church, for being a dear friend for better than 20 years. Thanks, Ellen, for reading my manuscript and keeping me biblically correct.

Rev. Care Crawford, Pastor of Congregational Life, Caring Ministries, she is by far the most inspiring speaking I've ever heard address a congregation, audience or a small gathering and stir emotions to depths of our being, through gesture, word, nuance, and the power of silence; while touching souls, with her soul. Care is a never-ending fountain of God's love and generosity. She is truly filled with the knowledge of the Lord's will, in all wisdom and spiritual understanding.

Many years ago, Gerhard Runken, my dear friend and brother in Christ gave me a gift of purpose, when he doggedly encouraged me to become a Deacon, which I dodged with excuses of being busy with things of lesser importance and consequence, than being a Bel Air Deacon; which is a privilege, an honor, and a lifetime commitment. As I reflect on times past, being a deacon is one of the most rewarding endeavors I've ever been part of.

Then there is Mr. & Mrs. Danny and Jinhee Pai Kim, two strong, young Christians, and Joseph Gentile, my long time friend, a Bible scholar and a man of strong faith whom I've spent many hours of Bible study, digging deeper into the Word. These people have true hearts for the Lord, and give credence to the words, "When you have helped the least of my children, you have helped me." They walk the walk and talk the talk. Their actions exemplify who they are in Christ. By association they have made me a better person.

And, a very special thanks to Mr. & Mrs. C. Fred and Susan Wehba, two very strong conservative Christians & my dear friends in Christ, whose generosity and hospitality has touched the lives of countless people. It is because of my association with the Wehba's and the other people mentioned earlier, that this book came into being, for my exchanges with them helped shape my thoughts through the sharing of Christian world views, and the need to share our belief in Jesus Christ, and the power of prayer.

Last, and surely not least, I'd also like to thank Rebekah Fear for reading and proofing the manuscript, many thanks and blessings to her.

DEDICATION

Heart's Song

From my heart I hear soft music
Songs that Angels used to sing;
Words that praise the joys of leaving,
Tunes that promise new born Spring.
Life Is surely worth the effort,
Sings my heart in metered rhyme;
Let our soul leap forth to action
And Break through the webs of time.
For Each start there is an ending;
For each death there is a life.
All Our time on Earth is measured;
Half is joy and half is strife.
Count The years that we were shackled,
Begs my heart in Lyric glee;
Join the Piper's dance of living;
Long ago we paid his fee.

In memory of my dearly departed sister, Geraldine
Johnson, March 24, 1975, the author of this poem.

FORWARD

All too often we get caught up in the frantic pace of this "Do it now!" "Get it now!" "Have more world!" Caught in this vortex of social and media pressure, we attempt to meet life's challenges head-on, alone. Doing that is a losing game, when we have the greatest power in the world available to us. Prayer! Why not use it?

The power of prayer is a gift from God. Make use of its supernatural sovereignty. As long as we look to our own resources, and ourselves we will always be restricted by our human limitations. But when we trust in God and in His resources, then we have His infinite capacities available to us. Apart from Christ we are weak, helpless and can do nothing. But, if we stand on a beautiful truth, one that Paul also discovered-- "I can do all things through Christ which strengthen me" (Philippians 4:13) -- then we are cloaked in an armor that can withstand the slings and arrows of the darkest despair. (Philippians 4:13) Apart from Him we are totally helpless and have no strength. Through Christ we have the power to meet any situation and overcome any adversity. In ourselves we are weak, but in Him we are strong. (2nd Corinthians 13:9)

Prayer is the only true armor we have against the adversities of this world, seen and unseen. Prayer is the most important gift we can give to others and ourselves. Prayer is a gigantic security blanket that protects and helps us get past our fears and doubts. Prayer is the warmth, which fills us to overflowing when all is right. Prayer should be the last thing we offer the world before we close our eyes at night. And, prayer should be the first thing on our lips when we awaken at first light. Prayer is the power that keeps the world and the universe in balance.

We must open ourselves, one and all, to prayer, and thank God for the privilege of prayer.

It is my sincere desire that this book will inspire you to live kinder, gentler lives, respecting others and yourself. This is a goal that is within the grasp of all of us, if we would only believe and have faith in the greatest book ever written, The Holy Bible. I urge you to look beyond that which is seen with mortal eyes and reach for the promise that lies behind that which is unseen. For in the realm of deep faith and belief, waits the pleasure of the Father to provide His children with all they desire; if they but ask.

Jesus impressed upon my heart, claim what you want by the spoken word. Do not say what you have if it speaks to a negative condition (poverty, sickness, fear etc.).

Only say what you want in your life. Stand on your word, without doubt, and you will have what you say. Man is a spiritual being, capable of operating on the same level of faith as Jesus. In Mark 9:23 Jesus said, "If you can believe, all things are possible to him who believes." And in Matthew 17:20, Jesus said to them, "If you have faith of a mustard seed, you will say to this mountain, 'Move from here to there,' and it will move; and nothing will be impossible for you." In Mark 11:23, Jesus says, "Have faith in God. For assuredly I say to you, whoever says to this Mountain, 'Be removed and cast into the sea', and does not doubt in his heart, but believes that those things he says will be done, he will have whatever he says."(So, pray the mountains in your lives away).

"Therefore I say to you, whatever things you ask when you pray believe that you receive them and you will have them." (Matthew 21:21)

If you want to be victorious, prosperous, healed or blessed give yourself over to the power of prayer, for all things are possible for those who pray and believe.

SECTION ONE

REALITY CHECK

Are you where you want to be in life? If the answer is "no," ask yourself why? Then get ready to accept the brutal truth. Like it or not you put yourself where you are, because of the thoughts you think. Thoughts are the most powerful things in the universe. They've led us from Neanderthal caves to the World Wide Web. Every object that has contributed to the growth of the world, as we know it was first a thought. Imagine a wondrous universe of unseen objects floating weightlessly in the ether, waiting for the first thoughts to be formed so that they could be made manifest, brought into being and form a tangible world of reality. If dreamers, inventors, scientists and engineers can construct innovations that have taken us to the doorstep of science fiction and beyond, by focusing on a single tiny thought, can you not change the circumstance of your life by shifting the focus of your thoughts?

Whatever your state of need, know that it is not greater than the power of God that resides within you. Prayer, coupled with right thinking and right action, is the key to your salvation. If the doors of life seem closed to you, blocking you from love, health, happiness, financial security, spiritual prosperity and emotional wellbeing, open them with the most powerful key in the universe: prayer. Remember, you have the Holy Spirit residing within you. Call on the Helper Jesus, left you, when He promised you, "I will never leave nor forsake you."

Know that God is in you and you are in the Father, and knowing this truth, put your dreams on the wings of belief and let them take flight. Accept the power of God and the universe and transform yourself with loving thoughts. And soon, you will put off your old self and become a new creation. Forget what you were in the natural, and accept that you are born again, into Christ, and your body has been transformed into a pristine temple where the Holy Spirit lives.

GUARD YOUR THOUGHTS

Thoughts! Thoughts are the most powerful tools in the universe. They can heal, help or harm. And coupled with the spoken word, they can tap into the laws of universal energy and move mountains with the power of God. That is why it is so important for us to stand guard over our thoughts. Only allow yourself to ingest things that are good for your mind, body, spirit and soul. Get rid of negative, hurtful thoughts, conversations, feelings and negative moods that are harmful to the mind and the body. When feelings of sadness, hopelessness and anxiety attempt to weigh heavily on you, dismiss them, by praising and giving thanks to God. --(Philippians 4:8) "Finally, brethren, whatever things are noble, whatever things are just, whatever things are pure, whatever things are lovely, whatever things are of good report, if there is any virtue and if there is anything praiseworthy-meditate on these things" -- "SCREAM OUT YOUR PROBLEMS" -- accept the reality of the circumstance, then focus your attention on finding what will free you from That feeling of helplessness. Over time the primary thoughts that we constantly entertain become a part of our lives, whether they are negative or positive, and shape our outer reality.

They become silent self-fulfilling prophecies. They guide our actions and attitudes and lead us in directions that allow us to bring oppression, fear, worry, ill health, obesity, poverty, confusion, weakness and spiritual death to defeat us. Or, they can uplift our consciousness and fill each and every area of our lives with overflowing blessings. Remember, "The way you live your day, is the way you will live your life.

In the following section there is a list titled "lifelines to longevity." They are things that will help keep you vital, mentally alert and connected to life. It is a law of nature that positive energy will draw positive energy. Negative energy will draw negative energy. And this energy, positive or negative, will manifest in the form of people, circumstances, situations and incidents that will be drawn into your life. So don't shrug your shoulders and blame misfortune or bad luck for the negative things in your life. Examine where the bulk of your thoughts lie, and the amount of fear and doubt you're lugging about. And, by the same token, don't attribute your good fortune and charmed life to "Lady Luck." Run a checklist of your belief system, and the way you embrace life, and how you deal with challenges. I'd be willing to bet you, at the end of your checklist, buried deeply in your subconscious mind, is a strong faith and belief system. And at the core of this belief system is a well of strong feelings that stirs you to know that you are equipped to face anything that is put before you -- "by His grace." And if those feelings could be put into words, I think they would be in the form of questions. "Am I being loving enough in this situation?" "Have I exhausted the billionth avenue that will bring success?" "What would God do in this situation?" None of this is new. It can all be found in the Word. The Bible spells it out quite clearly. To illustrate this point I've combined scripture and life experiences I've seen at work. Spiritual law is like seed planting and harvesting. The words you speak and the thoughts you think, like apple and grape seeds, will produce after their kind. So, if you are looking for health, happiness and vitality in your winter years, get involved with life. Don't shut yourself off emotionally.

You can choose worry, doubt, isolation, fear and defeat for your life. Or you can look beyond that which is seen and put faith in the promise of God. -- (John 10:10) "That He came so that we might have life and have it more abundantly". I choose to have fulfillment, success, love and happiness in my life. I think, feel, and breathe the fulfillment of my dreams awake or asleep, for it is what is behind the thought that counts. And, I know that fear and faith cannot live in the heart, at the same time. I choose faith. And, only believe that God answers prayers. So, I pray over and about everything. I do this because when my life is over, I do not want to be guilty of the sin of Prayerlessness.

FOR A LONG AND HEALTHY LIFE

Celebrate the blessings that life has given you by giving back to life through actions, thoughts and deeds. Here are some prayers, which have blessed me, and I pray that they will speak to you, and bless you as well.

"Prayers of Light"

Heavenly Father, thank you for covering my family and me with the blood and the love of Jesus, and for surrounding and enfolding us in your guiding, and protective white light.

"Wholeness of Life"

Thank you Lord for blessing each and every area of my life, with mental, emotional, physical, and spiritual well being, and providing me with financial security.

"Upon Awakening"

I give thanks for the breath of life, a safe passage through the night and another day to do Your will, dear Lord.

"Dealing With People"

Let me not go forth without Your hand upon me, for by myself, I am weak, prideful and can do nothing. But with You I can do all things, with a loving heart, that allows me to be less self-focused and more compassionate. With your strength, Father, I am less fearful and better able to see the other person's point of view. Free me from pointing a finger in judgment, while ignoring the three that are pointing at me.

"That Quiet Voice"

When truth prevails wise men listen and fools fail to hear it. Oh, Heavenly Father allow me to hear the quiet stirring within me which is so often mistaken for a hunch or fate. Grant me the truth, knowledge, wisdom and understanding to follow the Good Shepherd and to know His voice, so that I may not follow the voice of a stranger. And, forever let me feel the quickening of the Holy Spirit that dwells within me and keeps me on the narrow, less traveled path.

"Accepting God's Gift"

Knowing that I am created perfect, in the image of God, and given dominion over every creature of the Earth that flies, crawls or swims, why do I choose to step out of Your light, fall from grace and struggle through life, listening to the world, the flesh and the devil? (Psalm 8:3-8) When I consider Your heavens, the work of Your fingers, The moon and the stars, which You have ordained, What is Man that You are mindful of him, and the son of Man that You visit him? For You have made him little lower than angels, and You have crowned him with glory and honor. You have made him to have dominion over the works of Your hands; You have put all things under his feet, all the sheep and oxen, even the beasts of the field, the birds of the air, and the fish of the sea, that pass through the paths of the seas. (Psalm 8, cont.) I suspect that it is because of ignorance, a lack of understanding of the Bible and not standing on "the Word," that I do not fully accept Your gracious gift at all times.

"Stand Strong"

I pray that God will cover me with the blood of Jesus and give me the strength, to break the generational curse, that has for so long trapped me in the cycle of abuse, which cause me such, mental, physical and emotional pain. Lord Jesus, I pray that I may find the courage to stand up and protect (my body) the home of the Holy Spirit, and defy any abuse that would defile me, by speaking these words, "My body! My temple! It is protected from all harm." I have prayed aright and feel the presence of my Lord beside me, strengthening my resolve. Amen

"With Clasped Hands, Release the Holy Spirit Within"

If we would but look beyond that which is seen - the illusions of this secular world – and penetrate the haze of material confusion and fill our souls to overflowing with the warmth of God's unseen promise(s), how calm our lives would be. Then seeing with eyes and hearts free from doubt we would know that there is no lack, for our God supplies all of our needs according to His riches in glory by Christ Jesus (suggested by Philippians 4:19). And as the promise goes on to say, The Lord has pleasure in the prosperity of His servant, and Abraham's blessings are mine (Psalm 35:27).

Let us receive the promise of spirit through faith and step back into God's guiding light, for it is always there, ready and waiting for us. Utilize the greatest power known to mankind - prayer. Use it to transform sickness into health, poverty into wealth, doubt into faith, fear into strength. And never ever embrace and claim negative circumstances in your life in a possessive form. In doing so you accept ownership to the very thing or things that are holding you back and keeping you from achieving the life God desires for you. Jesus never spoke the problem: He prayed the answer. He spent much time in prayer. He did not dwell on present circumstance. He prayed and spoke the desired results. Should we do less?

"Move With Authority"

As sons and daughters of our Heavenly Father, we are vessels, spiritual beings having human experiences, put here for the express purpose of doing His bidding. As such, we are to be glowing examples to the world, not fearful creatures of little faith that view life's challenges as insurmountable. We are sons and daughters of the most High God, Heirs to the throne. We must stand on our Father's Word and exercise supernatural power to overcome any and all obstacles, for there is nothing greater than God. In our knowing, we realize another truth of Jesus' - "I am the way, the truth, and the life" (John 14:6) -- and we must move in that authority. (John 14:7) We also have the power to invoke the Spirit of truth, whom the world cannot receive, because it neither sees Him nor knows Him; but you know Him, for He dwells within you and will be with you." (John 14:17) Call upon Him and He will answer. "All things are possible for him that believes." (Mark 9:17-23)

Pray! Prayer! Constant prayer is essential when seeking a better life. And while praying it is very important to visualize your desires in all of their full-blown glory, not the situation that you are presently moving through. I am not saying to pray and sit back and let God and the universe heap your desires in your lap. Pray and be proactive and ever alert for divine intervention to step in and help you turn the right corner, knock on the correct doors, ask the right questions, and witness new avenues of opportunity as they open up to you.

In your waking hours constantly feel your better life building inside you. And if despair descends upon you, live the moment and let it pass quickly, knowing that it is only a temporary state of being. You could not prolong the minute that just passed. Nor can you hold onto yesterday's joy or despair, even if you wanted to. We only have the present moment we are living in. Why not make it the best moment possible. BE IN THE NOW! We cannot live in the future, for it quickly becomes the present. The past is behind us, and no matter how glorious it was, leave it behind where it belongs, no matter how pleasant the memory. Focus on making the present a wonderful now. The best thing that can be said for an unpleasant past is that it can be used as a life lesson. Let it help you better yourself, and learn to make wiser choices in the future.

"Give with a Healthy Heart"

On the road to health, happiness, and a better life, give comfort to others along the way. Never become so obsessed by the goal that you forget to enjoy the journey. Give with a smile or a glance. Offer a compliment or a silent prayer, in passing, to a stranger. They will feel it and pass it on. You may never know the power of the ripple effect that you've set into motion, but believe that it is a good thing. In the same way, a frown, an ugly word or foul gesture can ignite the fuse of hatred lurking beneath the surface, in this volatile world we live in. Hate mongers, like thieves who wait in the dark to steal, kill and destroy, prowl the streets of this modern day world ready and waiting to explode. We must diffuse the bombs of hatred and anger, with prayers and love.

"Take a Mental Shower"

Seek and find the best in others and they will (eventually) find it in you. Encourage and you will be encouraged. If you go around with hate, envy, anger, fear, pity and doubt hardening your heart, you will find those things at every turn, for subconsciously you are looking for and calling them to you. Rest assured they will be found and sometimes multiplied tenfold, for the law of energy in the universe responds equally to the power and strength of negative emotions, as well as to words of praise and hope.

It is a fact that we can always find what we are looking for, if we look hard enough. So why not search for things that will improve the quality of your life and the lives of the people you come in contact with. Clean the cobwebs of pettiness, nitpicking, faultfinding, gossip, pride, and envy from your heart. These are the tools of the devil's trade. They seem small, insignificant, but if left unchecked, they take root and strangle a Christ like heart, much like tares with corn.

Become a person of light who encourages without a word. Inspire by the inner light of faith, belief and the God consciousness that lights your way -- a light which sheds a glow on the things of good report that you allow your mind, spirit, heart and soul to dwell on. Let this light clear away the darkness in the lives of those who cross your path, and guide the way to the promise(s) of the Father. "I have come so that my people might have life and have it more abundantly." (John 10:10) Knock, seek, ask and claim the promise, knowing full well that the Lord's blessings will be heaped upon you, pressed down to overflowing.

Then as the Lord cleansed Israel, He will sprinkle clean water on you, and you shall be cleansed. He will cleanse you from all of your filthiness. He will give you a new heart and put a new spirit within you; He will take the heart of stone out of your flesh and give you a heart of love. He will put His spirit within you and cause you to walk in His statute, and you will keep His judgments and do them (paraphrased from Ezekiel 36:25-27). Then in your glory and joy you will continue to seek the kingdom of heaven, for all that you have been seeking is given to you by our Lord and Savior Jesus Christ, who is one with God, the creator of heaven and Earth and all that is.

"Resolve"

Be thankful for all of the worldly comforts that have been provided for you, but do not let them overshadow your higher purpose on this Earth. You are not your own, you were bought with a price (the blood of Jesus), and in the name of Jesus you offer service to Almighty God. Ask God to give you a heart like Jesus so that you may be His disciple in this world.

"First Light"

Awaken each day free of anger and regret. Before you climb out of bed to greet the day give thanks for the breath of life and another day to embrace the wonders of God's creation. And as you go out into the world be ready for the divine encounters the Lord brings your way. And as you involve yourself with helping hands and heart, ask the Holy Spirit to guide and direct your every action. When you move on, after letting the Holy Spirit guide you, you will know that you have served well.

"Driving To Work"

Heavenly Father, thank you for covering me with the blood of Jesus, and bathing me in your protective light, and surrounding me with a band of angels who will deliver me safely to my destination. While in my workplace, Father, give me guidance and discernment to do Your will, not mine, and to blend my work with the vision you have for me. Most of all free me from false ego. With this done I lay all of my concerns at the foot of the cross.

"Divine Encounters"

I believe there are no chance meetings in life, only moments waiting to be born, as I attempt to stay alert to the silent cries of my brothers and sisters in need. And when the appropriate words, deeds or actions fail to come to me, this I pray, "Holy Spirit, lay on my heart, what God would have me do."

"A Moveable Feast"

Father, give me the courage to be a witness. Help me usher my brothers and sisters into the house of the Lord, where they will be nourished and fed abundantly in "The Word."

"Grip of Steel"

Lord God, I pray, let my fingers grip my wrist with fingers of steel, when I raise my fist to strike the woman I love. Bring me to my knees, help me fight the fear inside, that cause me to take my failures, self disgust and hatred, out on my wife, children, dog, cat or anything that will not make me face the coward's fear that rages within my breast. Father, help me find the courage to confess, seek help to change, and put my self-hatred to rest.

"Advocates for Women's Rights"

As the Phoenix Bird rose from the ashes, and the spirit of Joan Of Arc, rose from cinders, I pray thee, to keep watch over these "Modern Day Joan Of Arcs" who are engaging in daily battle, for the rights of abused women, children, orphans, Common Law wives and abused men. And, like Saint Joan, I pray thee, Lord; lead these brave advocates through Divine guidance. But, unlike Saint Joan of Arc, these modern Day Crusaders, march against physical, mental, emotional, and spiritual attacks. They are not armed with swords and arrows; for their battle is not with abusive men, drugs and other substances that destroy; these vices and men are only puppets, with strings pulled by unseen evil. Their true fight is against the dark forces, the manipulators of this sin filled world. Our "Advocates", are armed with Holy Bibles, agape love and forgiveness. They are "Soul Sisters" offering "Soul healing." They are clothed in the full armor of God, as they do battle with the principalities that roam the earth, leading people into the ways of destruction. I pray you, Father God, surround these "Soul Sister Advocates" with a mighty band of "Holy Angels," who will keep them safe at all time, as they take their stand, against the wiles of Satan, as they do Righteous Battle for widows, orphans, and those who are unable to fend for themselves. Lord, I pray thee; keep watch over these brave advocates, for now, and evermore. In Jesus' mighty name, this I pray.

"Thy Will Be Done"

Father, so often we come to you praying for this, asking for that, always in a perpetual state of want. This day, Abba Father, I sink to my knees and ask for strength to do your will; to move forward knowing I will be able to handle whatever is before me. For You never give us more than we can handle. I accept and am strengthened by Your will. I am forged to perfection like precious silver and gold.

"Friendship"

Help me be the kind of friend I want in others. Let me be there to share a moment of laughter, a moment of pain, then use me Lord to help my friend(s) begin again.

"High Tea With God"

In my mind's eye, when I awaken in the early hours of the morning, I offer a prayer of thanks for my best friend, God. Then over High Tea in, the rose garden of my mind, we pass the time in quiet conversation. The talk is casual and relaxed. No monologues or eloquent prayers, just plain talk between friends. I listen, enjoying the exchange, and in the silence I feel His soft words of wisdom. I never hear a sound, but my heart fills with His jokes, laughter, and wise words of sound advice. I never see His face, we are always sitting at a lovely table, floating in the air, bathed in golden light. Then as always, when I drift back to sleep with radiant warmth filling my body and soul, I look forward to my next High Tea with God, my best friend.

"Heartfelt"

Thank You Heavenly Father for Your friendship and guidance. You know I appreciate all You do for me, though most often I take it for granted, never stopping to thank and praise You. So, now I offer these heartfelt thanks for being my very special friend and collaborator, in all of the things I say and do. And, so often I complain about how I look, and wouldn't it be great if I looked like a movie star, then I realize that I am a unique star, fashioned by the potter hands and your love, straight off of the potter's wheel, just as you would have me to be. So, forgive me Lord, for questioning your work of perfection...the one and only me!

"Soul Healing"

My spirit heard your clarion call emanating from deep within your soul. With eyes not my own, I saw the music of your need spinning, beaconing, bidding me come near. Your need was overpowering ...Or, was it --Our need? Wordlessly our bodies came together (in a soul healing hug), we held each other for the longest time, the silence -- soothing, healing, rejuvenating-- then our bodies, as one, swirling, spinning in a vortex of golden healing light, as God's soul healing hug enfolded us! In a blinding flash we knew, we understood... Now, when the world and its overload becomes too much for us to bear, we give ourselves permission (as you taught us) to step away from everything, close our eyes and move into the silence. There, I feel the warmth and radiance (God) of your golden healing light; as all fears and cares are left in the darkness, vanquished by Your golden healing light. I will draw wisely on the 2,000 hugs You placed in my God account, to draw upon at will. I thank You, my Abba Father, for providing me with this TRUST fund - one of many TRUST that You have provided for me. Amen.

"Wonder of Wonders"

Praise God for the life growing inside of me, may this blessed gift from God be made prefect, happy and whole. But, if this life growing inside, should be imperfectly perfect, I will love and care for this child with all of my mind, body and soul. And, in my heart he/she will be my perfectly imperfect gift from God.

"Shared Yoke"

Choking with tears my wife prayed to God. I, on the other hand, raged and cursed God! Why punish us with the daughter from hell, then Satan's son. We had spent our lives being good parents, good Christians. We tithed beyond ten percent, we are civic minded, we sponsor a Third World child, contribute to mission trips, and we are willing to die for Christ. A gnawing thought interrupted my rant, and shouted! "But, are you willing to live for Christ? Have you prayed? No! Then, fall to your knees, be accountable and share the burden of the prodigals!" They did not become Prodigals alone. Nor are you cursed for some ancient sin. But, you are being given a chance to free yourselves, and your prodigals. Get on your knees, and pray aright. Forget all the arguments, and accusations! Then, kneeling at bedside, tears streaming, hands held tightly, my wife and I entered into intercessory prayer. At first nothing happened, then months later a vision came while we were praying. We saw demons leaving our children, thundering over a cliff side, dashing themselves against jagged rocks below. We looked at each other and confirmed the vision, as being real. After a year of praying, praising and giving thanks to God, for calming us through 1000's of hours of prayer, we opened our front door, expecting Thanksgiving Dinner guest from our church, and there standing on the threshold was both of our prodigals, clean, sober and drug free! All thanks and praise be to God!

"Church Of Choice"

May the church of my choice be, the place where at sermons end I feel the presence of God, and hear not applause, or have the words of a pastors oratory being lauded and praised. In the church of my choice, I want to freely proclaim that my allegiance is not to this or that denomination (for I respect all houses of Christian faith) but, to God the Father, my Lord and savior Jesus Christ, the Holy Spirit and the indwelling Trinity. In my church of choice, I pray that I breathe, think, feel and give agape love to all, believers and Nonbelievers alike, for in my heart I know, if my love is pure and true, the trickle down affect will touch all of God's commandments. In my church of choice, at alter call, I'd sink to bended knees, and pray that God be by my side, every step of the way as I wind my way, through this minefield called life. For alone and by my own resources I am doomed, broken, destined to fail. But, by God's grace, I am more than a conquer! I pray Lord Jesus, You allow me, - a spirit Being, having human experiences - safe passage, less I misstep and have my spiritual soul attacked and blown to bits, beyond repair; by the lures and wiles of this popularity driven society, fueled to be more, have more material things, to be revered by the masses of this fallen world. Rather I'd die a mortal death, than die a spiritual death, which would separate me from my right relationship with Almighty God; my Abba Father. In my church of choice, I pray, that when the time of transition comes, I will be right with God, knowing that He knows, "I was never guilty of prayerlessness, the most dangerous sin loose in the world today. I pray, He'll know, that I prayed every step of the way. Amen.

SECTION TWO

A JOYFUL NEW YOU

We have spoken of the promise of your inheritance as sons and daughters of the Most High God. Now, let us examine the four basic principles that will change your life for the better, if you will follow them to the letter and pray aright. How quickly you will see a result depends on God's timing. Sometimes answers come swiftly, other times they come with the changing of the seasons. But, I know this, If you pray often and with deep conviction, knowing and envisioning the end result you want, manifest changes for the better in your life will appear like a seed planted deeply, one day a sprout will burst forth, then slowly, your new life will blossom like a flower. But, you must pray without ceasing, and stay in God's will, offering up your prayers in the morning and at night. If you go to sleep seeing the end results in your mind, those thoughts will filter throughout your entire being, and blend with your subconscious and be ready to guide and direct your every waking action as you move toward your desired goal.

Upon rising give thanks to God for delivering you safely through the dark night of the soul, and offer thanks for answered prayers; whether it is "yes." "No." Or, "Not yet." Then stand proudly and walk in the power and authority of Jesus as you move through the day, trusting His plan for you. If possible say your prayers at the same time of night and day. This will impress your desires on your subconscious mind and help you feel the power of God that surrounds you. The power and magnetic energy of God is always there, ready and waiting for us. It is the same power Jesus used when He came to earth to do His Heavenly Father's work.

USE THE POWER AND AUTHORITY OF THE
SPOKEN WORD

Ask Him and you too, shall receive. Jesus said, "Ask, and ye shall receive, that your joy may be full" (John 16:24).

It is the same power that He (Jesus) spoke into authority when He gave us the gift, saying, "These things I do you can do also – and greater." The Lord also stated, "Ask and you shall receive." But we are not asking. So, I urge you to speak your word with authority.

In the last section we talked about challenges that keep us down in life, things that stop us from letting go, trusting and letting God be God! In letting go and letting God lead, leave all control issues, and thoughts of detriment to others behind. You will soar high, on the wings of eagles, following the path the Lord has set for you.

Now we're going to talk about what to do once we've cleaned house and taken off the old self and put on our new self.

The Bible speaks of what happens when you remove an evil spirit from the body and leave that space clean... and empty. That evil spirit will return with several other evil spirits and take up residence if that clean space is not filled to overflowing with positive thoughts and actions. I personally like to call on the Holy Spirit to come forth and fill me from the tips of my toes to the top of my head, to overflowing!

And, when it happens, I get such a rush! It's a warm wonderful feeling rushing through me like the white water rapids; strong, powerful, majestic. This is another example of the power of God and prayer. So, we give praise, and exalt His Holy name on bended knees.

THREE KEYS TO SUCCESS
(Pray: morning, noon & night)

Now let's talk about three truths that will help break the shackles that keep us from good mental, emotional, spiritual, and physical health. To be free from fear, poverty, weakness, lack of faith and any other negative circumstance you want to remove from your life, remember Psalm 37:4: Delight yourself also in the Lord, And He shall give you the desires of your heart.

I. State your desires clearly. Tell God the desires of your heart and listen (God speaks, we hear, we trust, we act). Then set yourself up for success by directing your power, energy and thoughts to honorable pursuits. Surround yourself with positive, inspiring people. Make wise choices in selecting music, books, movies, magazines and television viewing. Live a positive life. See yourself living the end result of your prayers. Ingest only that which is good and productive. I'm not solely talking about food. This includes conversations, thoughts, gossip, envy and malice. "Let all bitterness, wrath, anger, clamor, and evil speaking be taken from you, with all malice" (Ephesians 4:1).

Find the good in people and all of life's circumstances. Say things that will uplift the human spirit and edify the soul, or keep silent. Nightly take stock of the day's events and give thanks for your many blessings. The power and the presence of God in our lives can come in the form of a smile from a stranger that lifts a sour mood. Or that angel in the disguise of a homeless person who merely asks "Please, help," motivating us to give out of a different sort of compassion, one which strikes a nerve and reminds us of our own hollow cries for help.

II. Confess your God-power. Step forward and state, "By the power and the authority of Jesus Christ and by His shed blood I confess healing in the face of ill health. I confess financial security in the face of lack seen through faithless eyes. I confess strength in the face of fear and despair. I confess God's guiding, directing, and protective white light, in the darkest of times, knowing that light will always dissolve darkness, and that all things are less frightening when seen in the light. Then seek, ask, knock and keep seeking, and asking and knocking until the doors open, revealing the answers you are seeking. Then give thanks for the truth that is revealed to you. It may not be truth that you desired, but remember, "Not my will, but thy will, be done."

III. Stand in authority. Feel the power of God within you. We were created perfect, in His image. But we often sell ourselves short, stepping out of His light, evading the strength and might of His healing power like frightened children dodging lightning bolts in a thunderstorm. It's time for us to accept God's gracious gifts. So stand in authority, feel, see and embrace your new life. Know that God loves you and wants to bless you.

Release your prayers to our Heavenly Father and remember Jesus' promised blessings to us. I remind you again Jesus said, "Ask, and ye shall receive (John 16:24). By asking you open the door for God to bless you as He has wanted to do all along. But you {WE} must ask. For He has given us free will. And, in that free will we must exercise the choice to ask. Humbly ask for help. Let Him do what any father, worth his salt, would do for his child. Help! Jesus said, For your Father knows the things you have need of before you ask Him. (Matthew 6:8). Pray always with thanksgiving, submission and assurance that you will receive what you are praying for, in Jesus' name. When you pray in Jesus' name you get exactly what He wants to give you, for you are coming to the Father in Jesus' name. No one comes to the Father, except through the son. So, if you {WE} preface your {OUR} prayer by saying, "Father I'm coming because you gave me authority in Jesus' name," you will transform your life and the lives of those that you are praying for. Remember, prayer will transform how you look at life. Pray often, not just when you are in need. Offer prayers of thanksgiving for the good, the bad, the ugly and everything in between. (Because we don't know what God's intention is, in having us face certain things) Ask God to direct your prayers. We may not know what hidden good is cloaked within the circumstance, which God puts before us, or how our prayers can help others. Be thankful that you are upright and still enjoying life, for every day of life is a joy, if you accept it as such. If you allow your spirit to reign free no matter the condition the body is in, then you can give yourself permission to love and accept every moment life offers you. And, remember you can give without loving. But, you cannot love without giving. Give voice to your desires, but leave room for God to work His wonders in your life, always remembering, "Thy will be done." (Matthew 6:9) For His visions are far greater than anything you or I could ever imagine. Always remember, pray first and then act, after asking the Holy Spirit to lead the way. I assure you that you will approach life differently, and you will be a much better person for it. Appreciate the new you, and take advantage of the privilege(s) of prayer.

MIRACULOUS STORIES OF FAITH

(Regarding the miraculous faith stories below) All of the situations depicted in the following stories are faith-based incidents, embellished to illustrate the power of prayer…with the exception of "God and the Butterfly," which is the factual faith-based journey of my nephew Michael; who contributed this story as part of his faith walk. His hope is it may heal a hurting soul.

"God and the Butterfly"

John Michaels was an angry young man, twenty-five years old. His life hadn't started out that way. No one's does really. The start of a new life is always a beautiful thing, no matter the circumstances. There is always a moment of joy. Sometimes that joy lasts a lifetime; sometimes it doesn't. In John's case it didn't. John had been angry for so long that he had forgotten ever being anything but angry. In fact, he had even forgotten why he was angry. He was just angry. All of the time, angry! His anger had led him to doubt the existence of anything good. To John, life was just a cosmic joke, with no punch line.

He, of course, didn't believe in God. But, how could he? To believe in God one also has to believe in good. And to

John, life was no good at all. He had turned away from people completely. Other than at work, he spent all of his time alone. Angry! One of the few things that brought John joy, or as near to joy as he could come, was riding his mountain bike in the hills. He liked to ride hard, work up a good sweat. Work off some of his all-consuming, ever-present anger.

On this particular day John rode especially hard. For this day he was through the roof angry. Why he was angrier this day than any other day he didn't know. It just happened that way sometimes. He rode to the top of a horse trail in Griffith Park, high above the city. He rode his bike in a gear not meant for climbing. He needed to sweat. He needed to ache. He needed to feel his muscles burn. When he got to the top of the trail he stopped, laid his bike down and sat on the edge of the cliff. He could see the freeway from where he sat, jammed with cars, as usual. He watched the jammed traffic. And he watched the trucks. And he watched the motorcycles. And he wondered, aloud. "Why?"

John wasn't sure what he meant by that. But he said it again. "Why?" And then he shouted it. And, then he screamed it, the anger in him boiling! He heard a noise from behind him. He turned, crouched like a wild animal, ready to attack. It was then that he noticed the butterfly, a very large Monarch butterfly. It was beautiful, a living work of art. Its wings were closed, and it just sat there; on a dead tree stump.

John looked at it for a moment, at first spellbound by its beauty, and then tormented by it. His anger quickly turned to rage. He noticed a large rock near his bike. He picked it up. He slowly approached the butterfly, the rock raised above his head. He meant to kill the butterfly. Kill this thing that so enraged him. Kill this lie, this false thing. Something so beautiful could not exist. Life was all full of pain and ugliness. This lying creature had to be destroyed. Within a foot of the butterfly John stopped, poised to bring the rock down upon the creature. He had to be quick, lest it fly away. But slowly the creature opened its wings. John thought it was about to fly away. But it didn't. It just sat there, its beautiful orange and brown wings spread wide, as if to say, "look at me, look at God's work. The artistry of it (of me), the Beauty of it, the order of it." John began to tremble and the stone fell from his hand. He fought to hold back the tears that seemed to come from a dark ocean deep inside of him. "I don't believe in you, God" John shouted! "I won't believe in you! I can't! I can't." And in answer to John's rage a voice spoke to him. It seemed to come from the butterfly, gentle, soothing, asking a simple question. "Why can't you, John? Why can't you believe in God?" And John answered, "Because I don't know how." And the voice replied, "Love. Love is how you believe in God." And with that, the butterfly flew away.

Many years later, on a Christmas Eve, John found himself living in a rundown, Hollywood flophouse. His life seemed at its lowest point, as did the lives of everyone else who lived there. As he sat in the window of his third floor room he noticed a butterfly gliding by his window. It was a large, beautiful, Orange and brown Monarch butterfly. It paused for a moment in mid air and turned toward John. "Love, said a voice. Love is how you believe in God." And then the Monarch butterfly flew away.

With those words ringing in his ears, John went to his old, beat up manual typewriter, and began to type. What he typed was a message of love to a hurting people, to a hurting world, to a Monarch butterfly. And, love to God. He went to a printer across the street, and with the last of his money, printed up five hundred copies of the message. And that night, when everyone was asleep, he slid a copy under everyone's door.

He then went out to Hollywood Boulevard and handed out the rest. The next day, Christmas morning, John was awakened by voices in the hallway. Gentle voices. Happy voices. Something not heard in this house of broken dreams. When he went into the hallway there were people, holding copies of the message, talking and smiling and exchanging words of Merry Christmas to one another. One of the people in the hall asked John if he had gotten a message. John answered, "Yes, I did. What do you think of that?" "I guess there really is a Santa Clause," the person answered. "Merry Christmas."

From that day on John's life was different. The low points were never quite as low. The dark times were never quite as dark. And though it would be years to come before John truly found God, he had found hope. The hope that maybe, just maybe, God does exist. And that He loves us all. And wants us all to love each other. I mean, if you can't believe a Monarch butterfly, whom can you believe.

These days John is a successful writer and an ambassador of goodwill, inspiring people, testifying and uplifting God's power, glory and benevolence through the written word. And as a lay minister he moves happily through all walks of life, spreading God's love; quoting, chapter and verse from the Holy Bible.

"Not Just Coincidence"

Peter was a forty-five-year-old purchasing agent and an active alcoholic who had lost himself in the bottle to the extent of losing his social graces along with his family (who continued to hold him up in prayer, with the fervent hope that he would beat his demon of choice-alcohol). One afternoon, over a five-martini business lunch, Peter broke a molar on a piece of stone-ground bread. Struck by searing pain, Peter was brought to tears and a conversation, which revealed a five-year lapse of dental and personal hygiene. Peter's companion was advising him to see a dentist just as Dr. Bill Butler, an orthodontic, stopped by the table to say hello to Peter's client/companion as he was leaving the restaurant. After a quick exchange about the bloody napkin and a piece of severely decayed tooth Dr. Butler left a business card and urged Peter to make an appointment, soon!

Peter agreed to the appointment, set the business card on the table and forty-five minutes later (and two more for the road) hurried off to a high-rise office building across the street, to his last appointment of the day. He had tried to cancel but could not because of poor cellular service in an area surrounded by towers. While rushing off the elevator Peter literally ran into Dr. Butler, who had been booked solid but because of a cancellation was heading off to the golf course. Seeing Peter's agony, Dr. Butler ushered him into his office, and after looking at his X-rays, Dr. Butler made him cancel his last appointment of the day. Which could have been the last appointment of his life. Dr. Butler performed an emergency surgery to prevent the poisons in a nerve from seeping into Peter's brain and killing him within the next week.

Later, Peter learned that his wife and her prayer group were deep into intercessory prayer for his salvation; just about the time he bit into his stone ground bread. They were praying for the Lord to give Peter a greater awareness of His power and His presence.

"A Life Yet To Live"

Childless, Sissy was in her winter years and carrying a change of-life baby, the last thing her late husband, Alvin had given her, before his big rig skidded on a rain soaked road while making a run from New Orleans to Florida, and ended his life in a watery grave. Sissy was a strong Christian and devout Baptist, so despite her doctor's repeated warnings over the years that childbirth could be fatal for her, she was torn over her untimely, unplanned conception. At a small church in the bayou, Sissy was held up in prayer by a group of "Holy Rollers," and her need for a healthy and safe pregnancy was held up in prayer for eight months, with nightly sessions of laying on of hands, and anointing of oil, by true believers.

Daily Sissy lived in the Word, dividing her time between teaching school, correcting homework papers, and tending her husband's grave, keeping it free of weeds and adorned with flowers. At bedtime Sissy would fall asleep with Bible in hand, praying for a safe resolve for mother and child, despite several near miscarriages. For eight months Sissy was plagued with nightmares of dying during childbirth and leaving a baby who would never know either birth parents. Or the baby would die in her arms during the first breast-feeding.

In spite of her gravest fears and the doctors' esteemed medical opinion that it would be sheer suicide not to terminate the pregnancy in the first stages, Sissy gave birth to a seemingly healthy baby girl, with a hematoma that should likely dissipate in time.

But in a matter of weeks the growth tripled in size. The prognosis was that it was a rare, inoperable, type of aneurysm that would explode without warning. Death was predicted to be quick and painless.

Not accepting medical science, Sissy and her church sisters shopped for a tiny bonnet and a baptismal dress for the ceremony that was to take place in 36 hours. They prayed, shouted, rattled tambourines, thumped Bibles, and looked to the greatest physician of all --- God. Then bright and early Sunday morning Sissy and the prayer warriors attended little Lisa's baptism and gave thanks for this precious baby in the doll-sized bonnet, a bonnet that was later worn by all three of Lisa's daughters.

"Who Does Your Hate Hurt"

Sheila Tipton, was young, gifted, and filled with a rage that shot her through Harvard Law School and to a job with a high-powered Georgetown law firm in less than five years. She came from working class parents and was always told about the things she could not have because she wasn't rich enough, pretty enough or smart enough, or good enough to get them. Sheila proved her parents and all of the privileged elite that had looked down on her dead wrong. She lived the American Dream, all of it. The top floor of a swank Georgetown brownstone, the best top-of-the line dream machine money could buy, a deep pockets six-figure bank account, and a stock portfolio that would have done the late John D. Rockefeller proud. At A-list parties Sheila found a deeper level of hate for the privileged elite. This hate, filled with passionate white heat, consumed her being when she discovered that she would never be a part of the old money inner sanctum called "The Elite 12" -- top social level event, party planning mavens, direct descendents of the founding sisters of The Daughters of the American Revolution.

Driven by a manic desire for a full partnership before 35, and a spot with the big dogs, Sheila would stop at nothing. Through backbiting, lying, cheating and swapping intimate favors, Sheila took on and vanquished all comers. An athletic, competitive A-type, Sheila always seemed to be running even when strolling, or when cooling down from her daily crack-of-dawn three-mile run in which she delighted in putting the jocks to shame. Breaking balls geared her for a long day of playing, down and dirty, hardball. Hearing them shatter was like the sweet smell of success.

Twelve-hour days were for wimps. Sheila and the late shift temp, Teresa, would burn the midnight oil until they dropped, sharing half sandwiches and cups of soup. Teresa was the only person Sheila treated civilly, maybe, because the girl was poor. And, seemed to pose no threat. Teresa was nothing, nobody, and someone Sheila could vent to without fear. The temp was like a maid, a janitor, and a service worker, seen but not seen, the fly in the room, someone of no consequence. For some strange reason, Teresa reminded her of her grandmother's patchwork comforter, the only thing that ever soothed her. She could say anything around the girl. The girl was "the fly" in the room, sometimes seen and heard but of no real consequence. And when Teresa's usefulness ran out, she'd meet the fate of all pests, a wet spot on the sole of Sheila's shoe. Seeing Sheila's self-serving tendencies, and leanings toward pathological narcissism, Teresa took her on as a cause. Nightly, on her way home, Teresa would offer prayers and light candles for Sheila at a neighborhood church.

In her off time Sheila targeted the social register, the blue bloods, she had been unable to penetrate since Harvard because of restrictions that still existed in her life and always would. They were emotionally fragile women living in glass houses, warped by a privileged, elite sense of self that repelled lesser people such as herself with nuances, gestures, and attitudes more repugnant than electrified barbed wire.

Their unbending rule of selectivity still brought her to tears; in secret of course. Her lack of breeding and a bloodline that dated back to the Mayflower was like a bitter curse. Thoughts of blood and ties to the founding fathers of our country, and old money families with music, science, and medical centers dedicated in honor of their memory plagued her waking and sleeping hours.

Sheila singled out "The Elite 12" and went after them with a vengeance, and through cunning lies and clever deceptions she wrecked lives, destroyed marriages and tumbled stellar careers with cleverly disguised gossip and unedifying words. Soon the once happy social group was infected by the rumors and at each other's throats with deadly intent, bent on destroying each other.

Consumed by hatred, Sheila imploded from the inside. Physical, mental and emotional breakdowns overtook her. Incident after incident turned the life of a vital, physically healthy young woman into that of a near, total invalid, and made her a frequent outpatient at nearby medical centers; before she was 35. How much did her hatred hurt? It withered her face, destroyed her mind, twisted her body, and put her into a walker when she became unable to walk half a city block without pain wracking her legs and back. Sheila's hatred became a cancerous organism, and manifested itself in her body and mind. It plunged her into deep silent depression. Black emotional states and strange ills held her mind captive. Ills that would release her for brief moments of lucidity when she received food and Bible verses from her only friend, Teresa, the temp.

A modern day Florence Nightingale, Teresa would bring food, books and music, and then when the fear of death began to plague Sheila, they would pray together. After six months of cleansing prayers and communications in which Sheila contacted and atoned or attempted to atone and apologize for her egregious actions, she recovered fully. Sheila prayed for forgiveness for her reprehensible behavior and the destruction of lives on her climb up the corporate ladder. She e-mailed her ex-associates and partners a heartfelt note from an anonymous author. "A careless word may kindle strife, a cruel word may wreck a life, timely words may lessen stress, a loving word may heal and bless."

In the months to come, Sheila went in search of Teresa, the temp, to come clean and concede that admitting the errors of her ways did act as a cleansing of her soul. And that hate not only hurts the hater, but the innocent as well.

Sheila never found the temp and no one could ever clearly describe her. But all those she talked to remembered the temp's soothing presence and radiant smile. And to the person they all said of the smile, "It was like a guiding light." "It made me feel comforted." "Like being wrapped in my granny's comforter, sipping hot chocolate."

"The Called Minister"

Early morning in a grimy Eastern, metropolitan city, shivering in near thread bear clothing a group of indigent men huddle around a fire in a 50 gallon drum trying to keep warm, while waiting at a day laborer pickup spot, all of them desperately hoping for a few hours of work.
Coat collar turned up against the frigid air, Moses Black, a gigantic black man leans against the side of a mini-market facing a bus stop bench and the street beyond. His lined face reflects a journey that has seen, first-hand, man's inhumanity to man. And depending on the weight that is bearing down on his mind he can appear to be forty or one hundred and 40 years old. At this particular moment he is 40 and engaged in an animated conversation with a friend only he can see. His mood turns serious as he whispers, "Bless me, God. I want every blessing you have for me. If I'm to be a blessing to others I must first receive the blessings of God. I thank you, Father, and I ask it in Jesus' name." Moses laughs then reads out loud from a list of things he needs to make happen this day; a job, some change or some kind of food to get him through eight hours

of backbreaking construction work. He folds the paper, puts it in the palm of his huge hand, then prayerfully places his hands together. With his eyes closed and his head tilted slightly toward the sky, Moses prays silently. A passing youth shouts to him, "Still praying to the Big Dog?" Never opening his eyes Moses responds, "24/7. And you should too." Then he hears the sound of a truck driving away from the back entrance of the mini-market with its rear door banging open. For some reason he opens his eyes and follows the sound. Before him is an answered prayer. A small box falls from the rear of the bakery truck. Moses moves with speed and agility after the truck. He scoops up the box of sweet rolls without breaking stride, and hails the driver through the side window. The driver motions for him to keep them as the door bangs shut.

Moses smiles and slaps Hi-five with thin air, "These are my favorites. I just said what I needed. And quicker than a New York minute, you made it happen."

Then, looking down the alley, he sees that his unseen friend is no longer at the bus stop.

Suddenly, Moses' second prayer moves past him, in the form of a man driving a pickup truck, bearing a sign on the door, "Jason Construction Company." The truck roars past Moses, moving toward a group of day laborers that are converging on it. Moses overtakes the vehicle. He pounds on the door with such force it shakes the truck and the driver Jason, scaring ten years off of fifty hard earned ones. Moses bellows into the truck. "Save a job for me. I work harder than six men."

Moses hurries after a troubled woman climbing aboard a city bus. He catches the bus just as it is about to pull away from the curb and muscles the door open. The driver starts to protest but wilts under Moses' hard stare. Moses spots his unseen friend sitting beside the troubled woman and thanks Him for providing the sweet rolls. The troubled woman squints at Moses and vents her anger. "Who in the hell is he talking to? It sure as hell better not be her. He don't know her." Moses considers this for a moment, and then concedes that he doesn't. But his friend does and He can help her with the stress that is killing her. Moses gestures to the empty seat beside the woman as the bus departs. He shouts for her to confide in his friend, and then follow the signs she is given. A middle finger thrust in the air! Moses watches through the window as the drama unfolds. He smiles and gives a thumbs-up to his unseen friend "God," as the troubled woman folds her hands in prayer and speaks quietly to the vacant seat beside her.

With the truck bed filled to capacity Moses presses Jason against the driver's door, as he sits in the cab taking up the space of two men.

The annoyance between Moses and Jason starts when the truck gets stuck in bumper-to-bumper traffic on a speedway. Jason is lost in a raunchy early morning radio program. Moses attempts to shut out the obnoxious talk show and focus on the pocket Bible that is all but lost in his huge hands. His three -- dollar bargain basement glasses are giving him enough trouble without the mind pollutants spilling from the radio. He casts a searing look at the radio that should have melted it. Determined to block out the radio filth Moses returns to his Bible. Unable the shut out the smut talk Moses shuts the Bible a tad shy of slamming it. The action and Jason's apology for disturbing Moses' reading pulls them into a conversation that reveals things about Moses. He is a "called minister," a gospel rock singer, a servant of God, and a man devoted to uplifting the human spirit. His ministry leads him to the tenements and the mean streets of the city. He takes "The Word" into the trenches. He's a smash it in your face, hands on gospel preacher, who takes on backsliders, cheaters and sinners of all shapes, sizes and colors. He specializes in tough love preaching, with a pinch of muscle to get their attention.

And, don't no night people, crack houses, gang turf, or funky bars, make no never mind to Moses. Where the voice of God sends him, he will go. And if he has to pound on a few heads along the way, so be it. If that's what it takes to get them to listen. Intrigued by Moses and the term "Called Minister" Jason presses for clarification. After a short silence Moses repeats the phrase "Called minister" as if he has never heard it before. However, by way of explanation he relates an incident from his past. It happened on a moonlit night. A mist of golden fairy dust drifted through the bars of his death row cell; "by the way I was innocent." Then the voice of the Lord, calling, pulled him out of a deep sleep and gave him a message. He was saved to do good works. And told to go into the ghetto and set his people free. You are to probe the ghettos of the minds, and help clean them up. And, those ghettos stretch from "Manhattan to Spanish Harlem!" Moses' booming laughter fills the air. Then, thoughtfully, Moses offers. So, therefore, "I am a Called Minister!" Jason gives Moses a look, but before he can ask Moses how he got off of death row, Moses laughs loudly and wagging a beefy finger. He lets Jason know that he won't reveal that. Not now, anyway. They lapse into silence. Moses returns to reading scripture.

They ride in silence until they exit the speedway. Moses closes the Bible and, never missing a beat, pick up the conversation as though it had not lapsed for a half-hour. The Lord put him on the path with a promise that he would always be there when Moses needed Him. That was twenty years ago. And his Jesus has never failed him. Moses don't want and Moses don't worry. "Look at the lilies of the field. And the birds in the air." He just listens to the Holy Spirit and goes where the light leads him. He needs money for his church of the Gospel. His congregation is mostly what folks call losers; gang kids, runaways, some battered women, and a couple of angry old folks. But he is reaching them through Gospel music, mostly Gospel Rock. His old storefront church is in ashes now, the victim of a hate crime, burned to cinders. Nothing left but ashes. "But them ashes belong to him and the bank. Hallelujah! For it will rise from the ashes, anew. Somehow. Someway it will rise."

At the job site, Moses listens to an inner voice which sends a tremor through his body, causing him to clap his hands, stomp his feet on the floorboard and break into a beautiful gospel hymn, which doesn't last long enough. With his hand on the door handle, Moses testifies to the power of God. God is the source of our strength. Prayer is the channel through which God gives His strength. This morning He and his brood, and their granny hen needed food. They prayed as a body of one. Then they laid their cares at the foot of that old wooden cross, and hit the bricks to do their thing. Tonight they will have supper. The Lord is something else. Or, as the kids would say, "The Big Dog delivers." This day His light led him to that particular street corner and Jason. "A Divine Appointment!" And Jason provided work. So in return Moses lays hands on Jason and lifts him up in prayer. "The Lord put Job through trials of fire as He has you. And, like Job in the end you will be blessed abundantly with great love and success." Moses ends his prayer, as always, "I thank you, Father, and I ask it in Jesus' name." Shaken, Jason spits gravel as he heads for the builders supply for materials, after turning over the crew to his partner; a recovering alcoholic.

That night while returning the crew to the pickup spot Jason steals glances at Moses, trying to figure out why being around this guy gives him a sense of well-being, when his whole life is going to hell; his marriage and his business are all but lost causes.

That night, as is his ritual, Moses stops by his gutted store front church, kneels in the ashes, and with a soiled gunny prayer shawl draped around his shoulders prays, "Lord, bring me into harmony with Thy will." Then, as in the early morning he lifts up his ghetto community and the world at large in prayer.

In the following weeks Moses proves to be as good as his word and then some. He constantly does the work of six men, exhibits outstanding leadership qualities and is a source of inspiration to the men.

In no time at all the radiant light that shines from within Moses attracts the members of his work crew to him like moths to the flame. And in no time he becomes the job site analyst. During coffee breaks and lunch hour Moses holds court for the troubled. He speaks in parables and cites colorful biblical stories with outrageous characterizations, which often fits someone on the crew. The stories always have hidden solutions to a bothersome incident that is happening in one of the guys' lives. They all marvel, in private, how his age-old stories offer solutions to their contemporary problems.

After the New Year, Jason is forced to shut down work on his housing development project because of a lack of funds. Then to compound matters, Jason's partner falls off of the wagon and Jason goes to the hospital. Stress and an old war related, back injury lays him up for an extended period of time; after having a radical disc surgery.

Moses offers to work for pocket change to provide lunch money and bus tickets for his brood to get to school. Then, on the side, Moses and the older members of his brood moonlight at the housing development site, and by winters end most of the framing is complete.

The bed-ridden Jason learns of Moses' midnight escapades from one of the female security officers hired to guard the development site.

One day in the early spring, after returning the work crew to the morning pickup site, Jason thanks Moses for the prayer he said for him when they first met. They worked. He's gotten a big job that's going to keep his company from going under. After an awkward pause, Jason offers Moses a ride home, so that he can get a jump-start on dinner. Moses informs him that he, Mrs. Goodlow and the kids don't have a home. They used to stay upstairs above his storefront church. For now they are living in an abandoned carpet factory. And as for dinner it's going to be easy. Now that he has a job they are paying token rent and eating bologna and Wonder Bread sandwiches, with cool-aid chasers.

At Moses' request, Jason stops at the fire-ravaged lot where his church once stood, and waits while the big man kneels in prayer, with arm raised to heaven while he smiles and visualizes his new church and gives thanks for it. While riding in the truck Moses describes the structure in such vivid details that when he stops talking Jason fills in the gaps. With a big smile on his face Moses nods and concludes the conversation. "Praise the Lord God Almighty, You see it too."

A short time later, Jason drops Moses off with the meager fixings for his brood's supper. He watches Moses duck into a thoroughfare then disappears into alley behind the building. After struggling with himself Jason exits the truck and follows Moses' route to the back entrance.

Using a big oil drum Jason spies on Moses and the brood through a transom window above the back door. He watches the preparation of sandwiches; cold-water bathing of faces and hands in a scum-coated sink. He then observes each child – in the glow-of a candle -- as they listen to grace being said. Most of them are bitter. Faces filled with consternation.

Jason's heart catches as he listens to Moses say something positive about each kid, chipping away at their defenses. After studying each child intensely, Moses ask the Lord for the right words. Words that will speak to his or her particular need. That something that is locked inside, bugging the hell out of them. That thing they can't talk about, because it hurts too much. For some no words come, only a hug. A hug that is first fought but gives over to clinging. Through action and words Moses knows he'll slowly guide them back onto the path of love and trust. The path they all walked as babies, before life betrayed them. A lump wells in Jason's throat as he listens to how skillfully Moses finds and points out positive things hidden in the worst events of each kid's day and finds blessings beneath the misery. Standing silently in the shadows nodding approval to his every word is Mrs. Goodlow, fondly nicknamed "Mama Outlaw," because she outlaws the tiniest of bad behavior. She is a runaway ex-school teacher, ex-valued person, ex-grandmother, who ran out of grandchildren to mother, and woke up one morning to hear her daughter-in-law and her son discussing what a burden she was. She packed her bags, slapped on her Cubs baseball cap, and hit the road with her Louisville Slugger baseball bat, with which she has been known to knock a mugger silly. Some B! Wanna steal her little money.

With the aid of two cardboard cutouts fashioned to look like the ten commandments stone tablets, Mama Outlaw laid out Moses' 10 laws (Or house rules), which she uses to keep the brood straight while their "Big Dog" is out bringing home the bacon, rules that keep the brood from playing house and getting into other mischief. No babies having babies on her watch! Thank you Ma'am!

A half hour later Jason returns with a truck bed filled with food and isn't allowed to leave until he hears Moses and his eight gospel singers rock the factory; and vows to let Moses work off the food bill.

Late Saturday night finds Jason at the demolition site of a new job filling the truck bed of a three-ton rig with pieces of good grade used lumber.

Sunday morning. Moses wakes smiling from a dream in which he was preaching in the new church, which he always visualizes. He saw everything in vivid detail.

Filled with excitement, Moses hurries through the predawn light to his cinder filled lot. Tears spring to Moses' eyes as he falls to his knees, hands clasped in thanksgiving, as he stares at the piles of lumber and building material stacked in the lot, under the watchful eyes of a security officer.

There is enough lumber to build his church and living quarters above for his brood. He thanks the Lord for his friend Jason.

Monday morning. Jason finds Moses at the pickup spot -- standing over the bodies of three old gangsters, administering in your face gospel. Shaking his Bible and daring them to move, he pulls a 14 - year-old runaway girl out of their van and gently sends her off to join his brood. Later, they'll send her home. Or get her into school.

As Jason watches, Moses stands the gangster against a brick wall and puts the fear of God in them. With his bare hands he all but destroys all the metal on the vehicle without bruising his knuckles. The display is an example of what will be their fate if he ever sees them trying to pimp another child.

On the way to work, Moses attempts to get Jason to admit being responsible for the lumber and building materials. All he gets is a wagging finger and an offer to be Jason's top foreman, with a possible partnership in the future. Moses accepts and succinctly offers his code of ethics. "Friends are forever faithful." Knowing that Jason is a retired Marine Corps officer, Moses gives him a snappy salute, removes his baseball cap and shows him the globe and anchor tattooed on the top of his bald head. He then explains to Jason that he was the gunny sergeant charged with the last wrongful death of a recruit going through Parris Island in the late eighties. Just before Moses was to become a "Dead man walking", the truth came out. They clasp hands and in unison shout, "Semper Fi, Semper Fi! Lord, if thy presence go not with me, carry us not up hence."

Today, Moses is totally involved with his community and the betterment of humankind. Aside from his church, he owns a community services center -- staffed by qualified personnel – where literacy, hygiene, birth control, social and job skills are taught to the underprivileged. And, as a servant of God his life is guided by the gospel, "In everything by prayer and all supplication with thanksgiving, let your requests be made known unto God." And as he discovered years ago, this truth is as true today as it was 2000 years ago. "I can do all things through Christ which strengthen me. Apart from Him I'm totally helpless and have no strength. Through Christ I have strength to meet any situation and to overcome any difficulty. In myself I am weak, but in Him I am strong."

Daily, Moses prays with confidence for God to bless him, to enlarge his coast, keep His hand upon him, and keep him for evil -- for this is the will of God for his life. If was good enough for "Jabez?"

"Book Of Records"

Cal came from a traditional West Virginia family. And like many Virginians he had a vast knowledge of his ancestral heritage. But, peculiar unto himself, he kept a journal in which he recorded his ancestor's deaths and their causes dating back from his great-grandfather to the present.

As a sketch artist, Cal traveled the world capturing and recording life's journeys in the lines etched in faces and hands of long-living people. The 59- year-old would walk the streets from dawn to dusk with sketchpad and pen, immortalizing the obscure and the famous alike.

In one inner-city ghetto, Cal noticed a grime encrusted, toothless, ebony woman sitting on a curb staring into the gutter. Cal sketched the woman's pus infected hands and weathered face.

Then drawn by some unknown force, Cal wordlessly emptied all of the bills in his wallet into the woman's lap and briskly walked away. Ignoring the money the old woman focused on the back of Cal's head with an intense energy that stopped him in his tracks. A powerful electric current connected them. Like a piece of metal drawn to a super magnet, Cal found himself, feet immersed in gutter slime, lost in the greenest emerald eyes he'd ever seen. For what seemed like eternity, he stood rooted to the spot, seared by an ancient energy flowing from the woman's eyes. Hunched over, inches from her face, he stared transfixed. Then suddenly her gaze shifted back into the gutter. Freed, Cal took flight, back to his studio loft, where he worked endlessly for six days and six nights, creating a painting he titled, "Black Madonna." All the while his thoughts were haunted by the words, "Blessed is he who considers the poor."(Matthew 5:3) Inspired by those words Cal created a series of paintings, which he titled, "The Enemy Within." The oil paintings were all of nasty angry cancerous red polyps. As a package deal, a major art gallery mounted a show around the Black Madonna and the polyps. A medical doctor bought "The Black Madonna," engaged Cal in conversation, learned about the words that inspired Cal throughout the creation of his exhibit and found them to be a cry for help. The doctor, a student of Energy Medicine and Intuition, explained to Cal that the word "consider" when translated into Hebrew means, "take thought for others." And the word "poor" when translated into Hebrew means "those in need." Searching Cal's soul through his eyes, the Doctor asked if Cal would mind stopping by his office for an energy test, just a simple form with a few questions.

En-route to the office the doctor posed the question, "what if it was Cal who was in need, not the old beggar woman?" Hours later the doctor removed five walnut sized polyps, from Cal, that if left unattended for another ninety days would have proved fatal. Cal noted the date in his book of records. In ninety days it would have been his sixtieth birthday, and the anniversary date of the deaths of all of his male relatives; arriving at their 60th, "Death Day!" Though Cal was fanatical about his checks ups the cancer was hidden behind his cervix, and would have surely killed him; Save for the prayers he uttered daily.

However, Cal never noticed the emerald eyes of the surgical nurse who assisted the doctor. Nor did he see the glowing golden angel, which hovered above the operating table and guided every surgical move with steady hands, and penetrating green eyes.

"Angel & the Baby"

Angel Ruiz was a seventeen year-old, demon possessed Mexican-American youth, living beneath the poverty level, with his grandparents (who were the only parents he'd ever know) in a gang-infested neighborhood. Angel was filled with darkness; hatred filled his black eyes, which he kept hidden behind black sunglasses, which he seldom removed. Angel stole things, frequented conjure shops, read Tarot Cards, used Ouija Boards and prayed to the devil, to hurt the man who laid with his deceased mother and disappeared. Angel had nothing, thought he was nobody, and hated people who had things. He was so filled with darkness, that on the sunniest of days, when he removed his dark glasses, Angel only saw dark, angry, storm filled skies. The more Angel hated, the more his grandmother would pray for him, until unknown to Angel, God was planning a better life for him, a way out, the Lord was bringing Angel a reason for him to use his brilliant mind for good instead of evil. As with many things in life, Angel couldn't see anything good coming from the news that a sixteen-year old American girl had a 2 year-old blue eyed, blond baby, and was accusing him of being the baby daddy!

Being a fan of trash TV shows, Angel demanded a paternity test, and went on daytime TV to prove that the girl was a tramp, and no way was he a baby daddy. Wrong! Angel freaked out and wanted to disappear, join the marines and get away from the responsibility of manning up, but during a dream a Holy Angel of God came to Angel and took him through a journey in time and let him view what his life would have been had his father hung around. He saw love, sunshine, and happiness as he looked at the world, through loving, God filled eyes. Then the vision was gone, and Angel was in the street, attempting to break into a car and steal a lap-top, Mumble something about not being qualified to find work and support no kid," when a voice said, "God doesn't choose the qualified, he qualifies the chosen." Angel whipped around, and was staring at the brightest golden cross, dangling from a chain around the neck, of a holy woman of God whose blue eyes pierced his soul, and would continue to pierce his being, during the months that their strange friendship was born (after she gave him her laptop, and invited him to her refuge "Safe Haven" for at risk youth.) Watching this woman walk with God and the Holy Spirit, Angel became hungry for her kind of inner piece, that kept her, and real Christian people calm, when the outside world was coming apart at the seams.

One night the Angel returned, and standing in a bright light, from which only his hand was extended, the Holy Angel asked, "Are you ready?" Without a word Angel took the hand of the Holy Angel and went on a crusade, with aid of his spiritual leader (the founder of "Safe Haven"), he takes on the world. He fights the legal system (upon turning 18) to gain custody of his (illegitimate 2 year-old) son, he fights for the right not to be in a gang, he fights to become gainfully employed, and he fights his inner fears to become the father he never had, and he wins on all fronts.

Angel learned contracting, built a home for his grandparents and his son, and became a man who leads by example, as he made a ritual of going to church on Sunday, praying over every meal; made a ritual of holding his son in his arms, looking into the sky proclaimed what a bright day the Lord has made. For Angel there are no dark days, for the light of the Holy Spirit within him Lights his path.

"The Power of Prayer"

Councilman Zev Berman is an honest politician, devoted to the people of his multicultural Mid-City district. A man with a big smile, an ever-available ear, and a compassionate heart, he is in tune with the needs of the people he represents.

But on this hot humid July night Zev Berman is tense, withdrawn and fearful for his district and the city at large. Escalating incidents of racial violence have turned the city streets into a powder keg that any small spark could ignite and bring forth a major riot.

During a volatile, highly charged town hall meeting Councilman Zev Berman is overcome by a tingling fear as he stands before a sea of angry, sweating ethnic faces, packed into the gym of a local high school. Shouted demands for immediate action to stop the rash of violent terrorist attacks on African-American, Jewish, Asian, Arab and Muslim houses of worship receive rowdy applause.

Civil conversation quickly turns into nasty vigilante threats that accentuate the demands to stop the bombing and burning of churches, temples, Synagogues, Mosque, and the armed assaults on day care centers. Pictures of chilling graffiti and defiled houses of worship are shown. Fingers are pointed, sides are taken and old hatreds flare up. The smell of revolt hovers over the overcrowded room as Rabbis, Moslem holy men, black Baptist preachers, Buddhist priests, Catholic Priests and Protestant ministers desperately try to calm their factions as name calling builds to the point of no return. Bloody violence is only a heartbeat away.

The survival instincts of the street people in the room send them fleeing toward the exits, as a free-for-all breaks out. The doors are locked, barred, from the outside! They cannot escape. People scramble between the savage brawl, looking for a way out. There is none. Seconds later a series of firebombs sets the building ablaze. Shots from the street riddle the building as the shooters hurl racial epithets. Access to the roof and a fire escape are cut off when a blast caves in the roof above. Minor injuries abound as plaster and old timbers crash into the room below as the second floor crashes down onto them.

Screams of panic and pain knife through the hot, humid night, and mingle with the shrill sounds of approaching fire and police sirens, and crackling flames. Building to inferno intensity, the rapidly spreading blaze pushes the occupants in the room into an ever-shrinking circle. With death imminent and the floor strewn with victims of smoke inhalation, a homeless man and woman join hands to form a circle of prayer. Reluctantly the religious factions clasp hands, leaving Councilman Berman to complete the bonding link; of reluctant prayer warriors, all speaking in the native tongues. Their voices rise from meek whispers to a powerful, rousing, house shaking gospel tribute to the glory and the power of the Almighty. Onlookers on the streets stand, stunned, as Arab, Buddhist, Moslem, Asian, White and Black voices compete with the threatening crackle of the flames. Then as if on cue, lightning and thunder fill the night. The thunder and lightning are quickly followed by a heavy torrential downpour of rain and hail that spills through the hole in the roof, blanketing the people below in a safe cover of water.

Bystanders on the street look around in confusion, as the out of season, torrential downpour extinguishes the once raging fire. As the flames are reduced to almost nothing, onlookers, police officers, fire fighters, and the people in the building sink to the ground with their hands clasped in prayer. Together, the survivors, offer a corporate prayer which drifts upward, into the star filled night sky.

"No Greater Gift Than Love"

Everyone in the Mission District knew them as the "Odd Couple." FM. ("Fix it man") and OMB (the initials were a heavily guarded secret) were the best of friends and the most unlikely two people you'd ever pair up as BFF's. FM was a big, Nordic-type Swede, muscles going to seed, a man given to mumbling to a locket dangling from a chain around his neck. OMB was a small, wrinkled African-American, who looked like a grasshopper and dressed like Jiminy Cricket, down to the derby hat, spats and cane. The torrential rain that came and went suddenly fazed neither. Nor did either notice the frail twelve-year-old youth with a handgun crammed into the pocket of an old, extra large army fatigue jacket, which all but hid his spindly legs. They were on a hustle with a single-minded purpose. F.M. and OMB needed money for soul-numbing cheap wine to keep their minds scrambled, cushioned against the dark thoughts which haunted them awake or asleep. But tonight they would have to face reality.

At precisely eight o'clock, in Bloom's Mini Market, their target for work when all else failed. FM started the chain of events as he dragged two garbage cans filled with the day's trash to the curb and stacked them in the gutter in front of the market. At that moment the youth with the handgun joined a small group of people watching OMB do a smooth soft shoe to the accompaniment of his trusty tissue paper-covered pocket comb. Lost in the music and the taps of the cracked patent leather shoes, banging out hypnotic licks on the chipped sidewalk, the youth stood enthralled.

Behind the crowd, Mr. And Mrs. Harold Stein, a dapper octogenarian couple, hurried into the market. Signaling the end of his act OMB spun like a spinning top, stomped his feet, bowed at the waist, tipped his hat and smiled brightly. He was rewarded by some change and crumpled bills as his audience moved away.

Inside the store the youth wandered into the back, crouched down and hid behind a stack of boxes, while FM and OMB counted the night's take and argued about what cheap gallon jug of wine would most compliment the box of moldy donuts they were eyeing as though it were a gourmet feast.

Lost in tearful farewells the Steins and Bloom were distracted, as the Steins shared their sad tale of woe. After forty years of business they were being shut down. The building has been red tagged for repairs and will be condemned if the structure is not brought up to code. Not a chance! The repairs would be too costly. Contractors are too high. They had to let go the last of their three employees. Their Goodwill-type furniture that had serviced the low-income residents for all these years would soon be a thing of the past.

Through a mirror mounted in the corner Bloom and OMB saw the gun on the floor as the youth stuffed every available pocket of his jacket with soup, cough medicine, soft dog food and lighter fluid. Knowing the drill OMB wanted to get out of there, and fast. They didn't need any more trouble. He tugged at his friends' arm as his feet moved him toward the back of the store.

Kneeling eye-eye with the youth he pulled out a handkerchief and dazzled him with magic tricks. Now you see it! Now you don't! The gun was gone from the floor, but Bloom didn't miss seeing it disappear behind the stacks of ice cream in the back of the freezer, seconds before the city's finest entered in response to the silent alarm.

The youth was searched and caught with the stolen items. But, with no weapon they couldn't charge him with attempted robbery; they didn't have time to search the premises. They were need back on the street. It was Bloom's call. Did he want the kid arrested or not?

Tears, coughing and nasal mucus came quickly… Through chocking sobs, the youths, explains that he can't go to jail. He's the only one who can take care of the family. They live in a wooden crate beneath a bridge near the dry wash. They are immigrants with no help from the city or the state. His grandmother and Jorge are sick. Bloom didn't have the heart to press charges, especially when FM and OMB paid for the stolen goods. As the youth leaves with the disgruntled odd Couple, Bloom tells the Stein's that FM was an excellent fix it man, in his sober days, and suggests they work out a deal with him. He could make their building good as new. And they'd spend next to nothing. The Steins offer a win-win situation. FM agrees to work for room, board and a small salary, only if he can make the same deal to any work crew he might choose to hire. A firm handshake seals the deal.

Later that night the youth, his grandmother and their three-legged dog, Jorge, moved into the building with FM and OMB.

Months later the building is transformed from eyesore to a thing of beauty. During the months while working on the building and helping the immigrant grandmother regain her health, the trio experienced a group "soul healing." FM and OMB get clean and sober, and the youth slips into an overcrowded inner-city school where his presence is never questioned in the classrooms.

To earn extra money to help feed a number of their homeless friends, still on the streets, OMB opens a restaurant on the ground floor of the building, and reveals the guarded secret behind the initials OMB. On Basin Street, in New Orleans, Louisiana, he was known as the greatest "One Man Band" to ever live. Then borrowing from a page in his life while living in Kansas City, where he was known as the king of "The Pig 'N A Poke Cafe," he converts a huge oil drum into a barbecue pit and brings to life a West Coast version of the "Pig 'N A Poke Cafe," And just as his motto in Kansas City, stated "If you can't pay for the meal you gotta dance with the monkey." And the monkey delights in making folks laugh while he teaches them soft shoe steps to dance away the blues when they gets too bad.

By the time the restoration is complete the entire upper floor of the building is filled with homeless people, sleeping on cots, and learning the trade of furniture repair and upholstering from the Hungarian grandmother who had once owned, and operated, a factory in the old country.

And, Albert Curtis, (OMB) from Sweet Parish, Louisiana, returns to his second greatest love; full-time master chef, of his own soup kitchen.

On the day the Steins return to their building, two serendipitous things happen. A postal worker and her supervisor who look suspiciously like younger versions of the Steins deliver a letter that announces listing of probate buildings in the area going up for auction. The second serendipitous thing is that the youth finds an envelope containing $500,000 in the seat of an old chair being prepped for re-upholstering. It is more than enough money to buy the building and provide business startup capital; for a few years if managed right. The youth's Hungarian Grandmother "yelps", "A few years! Ten years in my hands. And we make profit, like true American capitalist!" Bloom's Mini Market was boarded up several years ago after he and the Steins were killed in a police shoot-out involving a twelve-year-old robber. They chalked the experience up to alcoholic delusions or four restless souls keeping history from repeating itself... When all of the legal matters are taken care of, FM prepares to hit the road in an old Ford pickup truck, bearing a sign "Fix it man. I fix things others can't or won't." He promises OMB that he will return someday. Once bonded together by the pain of their grief, the loss of two generations of Curtis, when their parish church in Louisiana was blown away by a tornado and the strange disappearance of FM's wife, without a trace; now they are bonded together by a renewed love for God and humanity. They seal the promise with a bear hug then turn quickly away, hiding the stinging in their eyes. Short of a freeway on ramp FM fingers the locket hanging from his rearview mirror, stabs a straight pin in a map of the United States and takes off to find his destiny; with a prayer of thanks giving filling his heart, and, the hope that his wife is still out there, somewhere; waiting.

"False Voice"

It is a strange night. Things are in the air. Otherworldly beings are more active than usual. Uneasiness grips Andreas Pushkin as he sits behind the wheel of his cab listening to a Christian radio station, counting the minutes before quitting time. He has an urgent need to get home and call the prayer hot line. It is after midnight, but the line is active 24/7. All of Andreas' senses alert him that someone is in mortal danger this night, though he has no idea who. Gripped by a deepening sense of dread, Andreas pulls his cab forward into the glow of a street light and buries himself in the pages of his dog-eared Bible.

Then, clasping his hands tightly together he begins an intercessory prayer, -- as he so often does when he feels the menace of Satan stalking the night. Andreas speaks softly to, God, "I reach out beyond myself and pray, not for my own needs, but for the needs of those around me. I pray for my family, friends, and neighbors who do not yet know Jesus Christ. I pray for the needs of those in the body of Christ. I bring before God all the various needs of others that have come to my attention. And, I offer a special prayer for a soul that is in mortal danger tonight." With a heartfelt "Amen", Andreas closes his Bible, checks his watch and starts the cab, ready to call it a night. The dispatcher's voice crackles through the radio, sending chills through Andreas' body, as he's given orders to pick up a fare on the "North Side." The driver that usually handles that side of town is out sick.

On the way, to pick up his fare, Andreas recalls the history of racism which permeates the area he is heading into. The unwritten law there is that all foreigners and people of color best beware. This is white man's territory.

He parks in front of a seedy bar, where his fare waits, fighting a gut wrenching fear of entering the bar unaware that he is fearing for his own safety.

After aborting the urge to put the pedal to the metal and get the heck out of there, Andreas finds himself standing inside the dim, rancid smelling, smoke filled bar, silently blanketing himself with a prayer of protection; praying to be protected by Jesus' white light.

Andreas squints through the haze, focuses on the bartender and several people in the rear of the room, all watching a wall mounted television set.

A feeling of abject malevolence repels him as he moves, hesitantly, toward a Skinhead -- sitting alone -- engaged in an angry conversation with no one but the demons that lurk in his alcohol soaked brain. Andreas' fear and disgust try to force him to turn and leave this vile place. But, he is compelled to look at the Skinhead. Suddenly the Skinhead angrily slams his fists down on the bar, revealing the words "kill" and "hate" tattooed across his knuckles. Then the sight of "666" and the pentagrams tattooed on the man's cheeks confirms, for Andreas, that this is not the place for him to be.

A quick exchange of words with the bartender and the patrons -- who glare at his swarthy complexion -- verifies that none of them called for a cab. Andreas makes a quick exit out the side door. When he comes to the front of the bar he notices the Skinhead standing near his cab, weaving drunkenly, on unsteady legs. Andreas hears a hollow voice. The voice says, "He is not one of God's children. He is filled with hate. He tattoos it on his fists. He wears the sign of Satan, "666," boldly across his forehead. He is My enemy." But, Andreas is compelled to approach the Skinhead, disobeying what he thinks is the voice of God and asks the Skinhead if he needs a ride somewhere.

A short time later, Andreas finds himself aimlessly driving about the city, the Skinhead slouched in the backseat, still muttering, to his demons. Suddenly the icy fingers of dread clutch Andreas. He realizes that the stranger in danger, this night, is himself. By disobeying the voice of God, by letting this Skinhead, this cesspool of hate into his cab, he has put himself in mortal danger. Andreas starts to pull the cab to the curb and order the Skinhead out, prepared to fight for his life if need be, when he locks eyes with the troubled young man in the rear view mirror. Andreas speaks to the Skinhead for the first time, since being ordered to circle a strip bar, until it closes. "This makes no sense. You're running up a huge bill. Give me a destination or get out." The Skinhead replies, "Anywhere's fine. Anywhere at all." Andreas pulls into the nearest curb and stops. The Skinhead slips him a large bill, and exits telling him to keep the change. Andreas hands the Skinhead a card with the prayer hot line phone number on it.

Andreas knew he was doing this in defiance of the voice of God, but felt he had to. The Skinhead takes the card, looks at it, crumples it in the hand with "hate" tattooed across the knuckles, and disappears into the fog.

That night, at bedtime, Andreas completes his nightly prayers and slips under the covers. Just as he works his head into the comfortable deep sleep position, nestled in the folds of his pillow, the Skinhead comes into his mind. On his knees, beside his bed, hands folded in prayer, Andreas hears the words, "Don't pray for him, God's going to be unhappy with you." Fearfully, Andreas looks around, then writes the voice off to nerves, lowers his head and opens his mouth to pray, when his mind is flooded with impressions, word pictures of God's wrath speed through his mind. Heaven parts spitting flames. Fiery eyes shoot yellow flames through black clouds, charring Andreas' body where he kneels. Strong hands lunge out of an angry red sky, and snap his neck. But, Andreas prays for the Skinhead anyway. And he also prays for forgiveness from God for himself, for disobeying God's command. For praying for one whom, according to God's own voice, did not deserve prayer. Out of the corner of his eye Andreas catches a glimpse of serpent in the branches of the Tree of Life, hissing; looking as though it's smiling. Andreas looks. The room is empty.

Several months later, the incident with the Skinhead all but forgotten, Andreas picks up a fare hailing his cab from a street corner. The passenger is a handsome, congenial young man, wearing a three-piece business suit -- carrying a briefcase. As Andreas pulls into traffic he asks the passenger's destination. Smiling broadly, the young man gives the address to, "The Victory Outreach Center" and says, "Thanks to you." Andreas is taken aback. Blatantly the young man says, "You don't remember me, do you?" Thoroughly puzzled, Andreas answers, "I can't say that I do." The young man tells Andreas that he picked him up outside of a North Side bar several months ago. He was a confused "soul" at that point in time. But, by God's grace, Andreas handed him a business card -- with the number of a prayer hot line on it. Until that moment the only thing anyone had ever handed him was a hard time. That night he called the number and found Jesus. Now he is gainfully employed (with hair and sans tattoos) and works a as volunteer with The Victory Outreach Center in their gang intervention program.

That night as Andreas says his prayers before bedtime; he adds a special prayer of thanks to God. He realizes that voice he heard those months ago; telling him not to pray for the Skinhead was a false voice, the father of lies, and the voice of human fear, fear of someone different, fear of strangers, fear of self. Then Andreas realizes, that God would never tell him not to pray for someone. Not even his most bitter enemy. For in the eyes of God there are no enemies, only souls in need. Andreas drifts off to sleep praying, "I do follow the good Shepherd and I know His voice and the voice of a stranger I will not follow" (John 10:4-5).

SELECTED BIBLE VERSES AND THOUGHTS TO STRENGTHEN WHEN IN NEED

⤬

"I have been through the valley of
weeping, the valley of sorrows and
pain. But the God of all comfort was
with me, at hand to uphold and
sustain Me." – Anon

⤬

A good friend shares the good times
as well as the bad.

⤬

"One little sin, what harm can it do?
Give it free reign and soon there are
two. Then sinful deeds and habits
ensue - Guard well your thoughts,
lest they destroy you." - D. De Hann
- Taken from Our Daily Bread,
poem by Dennis J. DeHaan, © 1997
by RBC Ministries, Grand Rapids,
MI. Reprinted by permission. All
rights reserved.

⤬

"It was only a brief little note, or a
word that was prayerfully spoken,
yet not in vain, for it soothed the
pain of a heart that was nearly
broken." – Anon

Appreciate the differences in people and have the wisdom to grow with each human exchange.

The fear of the Lord is the beginning of knowledge, but fools despise wisdom and instruction. (Proverbs 1:7)

"Lord, help me make my witness clear, and labor faithfully, so friends and neighbors turn to Christ Through what they hear from me." – Anon

Share the music of life that beats within your soul, with a world of new friends, let in by the twinkle in your eyes.

This Book of the law shall not depart from your mouth, but you shall meditate on it day and night, so that you may be careful to do according to all that is written in it: for then you will make your way prosperous, and then you will have success. (Psalm 1:1-6)

Color your world with pictures and thoughts of beauty, harmony and love.

Chances to be kind are never hard to find. Open your eyes and your heart. They're everywhere.

Bless The Lord at all times; And keep His praise continually in my mouth (Psalm 34:1).

Know there is goodness in the hearts of others, and seek to share yours with them.

Give to those in need it makes the spirit richer.

Keep your tongue from evil, and your lips from speaking deceit (Psalm 34:13).

Every word we say is released to the universe forever. Let them be positive.

God speaks through His word to those who listen with their heart(s).

The eyes of the Lord are toward the righteous, and His ears are open to their cry.

The greatest gift is one given with a joy-filled heart.

Better to be a selfless philanthropist than a self-seeking opportunist.

Negative acts and negative thoughts originate in fear. When we are motivated by fear, false gods and all that they represent can easily seduce us.

Thank you, dear Lord, for giving my son a strong self-image and the strength and power to surround himself with positive forces in his life, and things that work toward his greater good. At all times allow him to move in peace and harmony.

May respect, joy, health, long life and great success, and salvation be his all the days of his life and beyond. For now and forever he is bathed in Your guiding light and surrounded by angels.

Thank You, precious Jesus, for blessing my daughter with a healthy self-image and bestowing upon her the strength and power to choose wisely the people she has around her.

Bless her gentle soul and allow
streams of peace, health, harmony,
joy and respect, and success to flow
smoothly through all the days of her
life and beyond. And ever surround
her with a band of angels to hold her
in Your radiant protective light.

⚝

"Not in having or receiving, but in
giving, there is bliss; He who has no
other pleasure even may rejoice in
this." - Anon.

⚝

The Lord is near to the broken-
hearted, and saves those who are
crushed in spirit.

⚝

Thankfulness begins with a grateful
heart.

⚝

The beginning of thankfulness starts
with a good memory.

⚝

Stand for what's right, or fall with
what's wrong.

⚝

"Repentance is to leave the sin that
we had loved before, and showing
we are grieved by it by doing it no
more." – Anon

Don't wait to speak words of
kindness; you never know how soon
it will be too late.

Many are the afflictions of the
righteous; But the Lord delivers him
out of them all.

Delight yourself in the Lord: And He
will give you the desires of your
heart. (Psalm 37:4)

Do not fret because of evildoers. Be
not envious toward wrongdoers. For
they will wither quickly like grass,
and fade like green herb.

The key to growth is an honest daily
competition with ourselves.

Commit your way to the Lord, trust
Him, and He will do it.

Trouble and the strength to bear it
are both ministered to by God's
grace.

No evil will befall you, nor will any plague come neigh your dwelling. (Psalm 91:10)

The Lord will give His angels charge concerning you, and they will bear you up in their hands, lest you strike your foot upon a stone.

(Matthew 4:6)

Stand on the Word: Strengthen your life.

Call on the Lord and He will answer you. (Psalm 55:16)

He who dwells in the shelter of the Most High will abide in the shadow of the Almighty.

(Psalm 91:1)

Strive to stay in harmony internally and externally.

Never look at a task as too small to give it your all. It may be a mustard seed in disguise.

The mind of man plans his way, but
the Lord directs his steps.

When man's ways are pleasing to the
Lord, He makes even his enemies to
be at peace with him.

(Proverbs 16:7)

Angels of God touch the lives of
prayerful people as they do the work
of God.

Better is a little with righteousness
than great income with injustice.
(Proverbs 16:8)

Seek ye first His Kingdom and His
righteousness; and all things shall be
added to you.

(Matthew 6:33)

Speak with care the words you
would share. For they can help or
hurt.

Ask, and it shall be given to you:
seek, and you shall find; knock, and
it shall be opened to you, for
everyone who asks receives, and he

who seeks finds, and to him who
knocks it shall be open. With men it
is impossible, but not with God; for
all things are possible with God.
(Matthew 7:7)

⁓

Live life well and leave no regrets.

⁓

Hear the needs of others as though
they were your own.

⁓

Keep your inner rhythm flowing as
smoothly as a clear mountain stream.

⁓

There is beauty in all things, if we
look with unbiased eyes.

⁓

Feel your dreams into reality. Strive
to keep balance in all things.

⁓

For everything created by God is
good, and nothing is to be rejected, if
received with gratitude; for all is
sanctified by the word of God and
prayer.

⁓

Heaven and Earth will pass away,
but My words will not pass away.
(Matthew 24:35)

Let all houses of God unite and be as
one, as we practice racial harmony
and love with the whole family of
Man. For we are all fishers of men,
working toward the same end.

And as for you, the anointing which
you receive from Him abides in you,
and you have no need for anyone to
teach you; but as His anointing
teaches you about all things, and is
true and is not a lie, and just as it has
taught you abide in Him.

Never search for the right words;
speak the truth of your heart.

Whatever we ask we receive from
Him, because we keep His
commandments and do the things
that are pleasing in His sight. And
this is His commandment that we
believe in the name of His Son Jesus
Christ and we love one another, just
as He commands us.

And we have come to know and
have believed the love, which God
has for us. God is love, and the one
who abides in God, and God abides
in him.

In all your ways acknowledge the
Lord, and He will make straight your
path. (Proverbs 3:6)

We love, because He first loved us.
If someone says, "I love God" and
hates his brother, he is a liar; for the
one who does not love his brother
whom he has seen, cannot love God
whom he has not seen. (1 John 4:20)

Be renewed in the spirit of your
minds and clothe yourselves with the
new self, created according to the
likeness of God in true righteousness
and holiness. (Ephesians 4:23-24)

Seek the world of knowledge at the
feet of the Holy Spirit, our ever-
present teacher.

Beloved, I pray that all may go well
with you and that you may be in
good health, just as it is with your
soul. (3 John 1:2)

In business and personal affairs work
toward an end that will produce the
greatest good for all concerned.

Love is patient; love is kind, it bears all things, believes all things, hopes all things and endures all things. (1 Corinthians 13:4)

Today's dreams are tomorrow's reality. So, dwell not on sadness and suffering.

Think thoughts of your highest purpose and allow them to fly to you on the wings of the Highest Authority.

SECTION THREE

FROM THE HEART

For those looking toward the "Winter Years," and those who think the glass is half empty, I invite you to take a journey with me, regardless of your religious persuasions, for these thoughts are universal and embody the feelings, the thoughts and needs of the entire Family of Man.

Some of the things in the pages to come may seem familiar, or repetitious. And, so they are. I have reworded them slightly. But, as I feel that they are vitally important points I have an urgent need to reemphasize them.

I would like to share with you a quote that I often call upon when I lose my bearings and begin to despair.

"The future belongs to those who believe in the beauty of their dreams." -- Eleanor Roosevelt.

Now, to take some of my own advice, I'll stop searching for the right words, and let the truth of my soul's journey ring free.

I reach out to you with my heart, for I have been to many of the dark and lonely places I speak of in this section. The things I will share with you helped me climb out of the pit of loneliness and despair. So, let us begin this journey toward brightness, clarity and freedom from the grip of fear, despair.

THOUGHTS AND ACTIVITIES THAT HELPED ME
OVERCOME

"Rise With Joy"

Thank you Heavenly Father, for another day. The good clean clear breath of life, and perfect health. Thank you for giving me the Holy Spirit, to be leader of my life, the Lord of the harvest, my teacher, counselor and my guide. Let the Holy Spirit guide and direct my every word, thought, action and deed this day, as I meet every divine encounter.

And, Heavenly Father, let me die again to self this day and be born unto Christ, freed from ego and self-driven way. Let my living spirit reach out to the spirit of the Living God Emmanuel, and be transported through this day, and this life.

"The Dark of Night"

Feeling old, lonely and alone, tormented by regrets of a misspent life, I tossed and turned, caught in the grips of another, (sweat-filled) restless sleep. Swimming across the landscape of my mind, I saw myself struggling through howling winds, and swirling snow, clawing my way through the dark valley of despair. Aching from every limb, burdened with fear, bankrupt of spirit, I lay my head down, ready to welcome the eternal sleep.

But whispering in my ear was an, ever-so soothing voice, urging me onward, forcing me to my hands and knees. The melodious tones were like silken threads that kept pulling me upward, toward a distant, unseen mountain summit.

Still beaten down. Lost, lonely, afraid, suddenly something died within my chest-the last of life's breath. My spirit drifted away, in an ice blue, willowy wisp of vaporous smoke. I fell to the snow for the final time, fingers bloody and raw to the bone. Then in the last throes of life I thrust my arms to the heavens and wailed heavily my deepest despair. It was a baleful cry of loss, a feeling of being forsaken. Words and prayers escaped me.

Then suddenly a distant glimmer of light cut through the stormy night, guiding my way to the summit high. With renewed faith, belief, hope and purpose, I clawed and fought my way out of the pit of despair, to a distant light; golden and fair.

And, there in the new fallen snow, of the second half of my life, was "Winter Love," the golden flower of happiness, like a beacon to light my way, an omen to guide and bless the remainder of my days. As I look back it was a prophetic dream filled with signs and wonders.

The following are my thoughts and reflections, from that dream so long ago, for people who think that the glass is half empty, swirling with loss, misery and regret. And, to them, maybe it is so.

If that's the case why not empty the contents and pour in an equal measure of joy? Read on if you want to live happy, enriched lives – lives that can only be fulfilled by releasing the joy that lives within all of us; waiting to be set free! The joy that comes from truly loving and appreciating all of the wonderful things that life offers us. But, first, we must relearn or learn to like, love and appreciate who we are. Or, more importantly, who we can be.

"Winter Love"

The beautiful thing about the "Winter Years" is that we have made it through the growing pains of the first half of our lives and have gone through a lot of "been there," "done that" moments. We have been married, and had families, or not. We have felt love, loss and joy, no matter how fleeting. Suffered sorrows and deep wounds. In short, we have experienced a lot of "life."

But, in so many instances the circumstances we have experienced and gone through are not exactly the passages we would have chosen to experience in order to arrive at this point in time. Many of us are filled with remorse, bitter regret and carry blame as if it were a Red Badge of Courage. It is not! It is only excess baggage. And so often we reinforce those issues of blame and misery with resentments of things long past; churning ugly memories over and over like dirty clothes in a washing machine. Frequently agitating us. We keep this pain fresh and alive by frequently revisiting hurtful moments and reliving them in our mind's eye. We often qualify our stalemates and justify our inability to move on with our lives, by making excuses, such as: if I had, had the insight, free will or presence of mind, or the mature understanding of who I would be at this point in life, I would have made better choices. Then we cop out with a multitude of excuses: life gave me a raw deal; if it wasn't for my parents; I wasn't born with a silver spoon in my mouth. Being a minority has kept me back. There's still a glass ceiling for women in the business world. I don't care what they say! Being left-handed, and a "Ginger" (redheaded) forget it! No place for poor, uneducated folks 'cept on welfare. Forget being small or handicapped. We are the real minorities.

These are famous last words we've all heard. Well to them I say, we are all in a minority of some sort or the other. You can stay at the pity party or buy a ticket and join the dance of life. It can be a romantic, flowing ballroom dance, or a hot pulsating Salsa dance. It is your choice.

I assume that we are on the same page; otherwise your closing this book, and moving onto other interests would silence my voice.

I'm glad you're still with me, because I'm big on feeling good and sharing things that will help others feel good too. So, let's start exchanging ideas. The very first thing I learned about feeling good is that you can feel good if you want to.

It is the same way with feeling bad. You can accept a bad turn of circumstances, and make it into a day, a week, a month, or a lifetime of wallowing in something that is all but forgotten, by everyone except you.

No one can force you to feel good if you don't want to. It is the same way with liking ourselves or loving ourselves for that Matter. No force on earth, outside of yourself, can make you like, or respect who or what you are.

However, there are some people or events that can inspire you to take action. If you don't care for the person you see when you look in the mirror, look deeper because he or she is not the culprit who is causing your disease (disease). Believe me when I tell you, it is your inner self that you are having trouble with. Being the person you want to be starts by realizing that change comes from within. It's an inside job. So look past that image that you see staring back at you from the mirror and peer into that silent place within the stillness of your being. There, swirling around, in a murky vortex of confusion, you will find a lifetime of doubts, fears, insecurities, and issues of self-worth. Locked away in a vault of human heartache, these are the things that hold us back, and keep us from going forward, and allowing the bigger self, the bigger you, to emerge. Change cannot occur, until we take a good look at ourselves, examine the unfavorable things that we see, and start weeding them out.

Don't think it's going to be easy. It'll be a bittersweet, love hate struggle. But, I started to find faith and hope, when I stopped frowning at the world, and ventured a timid smile, and a WORLD of strangers on the street started smiling back.

Here is where the fun begins. Imagine having a mental garden hoe at your disposal. Use it to clean out that briar patch of detrimental thoughts, ideas and impressions you have about yourself spinning around in your head. Use it to till the fertile soil of your mind, to plant positive, rich new images and ideas about yourself. Stand guard over your mind, and whenever a negative thought rears its ugly head, pick up a mental watering can, and douse it with positive thoughts, newly planted in the rich, fertile, soil of your mind. Once this is done, get on with your life. And believe me, without a doubt, positive changes can and will happen in your life. Like you are what you eat. We become what we think!

Keep focused on positive things, leaving no time for harmful moments of reflection. It is a known fact that the things we dwell on manifest themselves in our lives. They appear on three levels -- emotional, mental, and physical. Make positive thinking second nature, and see what happens. I'm not saying to stop being a realist. What I am saying is to focus on finding solutions to effect positive change, avenues to help you get rid of the unwanted things in your life. I rarely say "your problem" or "my problem" for that denotes ownership of a negative condition. Let us look beyond the seen to the unseen.

Always cast your eyes toward the promise. That is what the great minds of our time have done and are doing. Everything that we have in the way of technology and household goods started out as a vague thought in someone's mind until their belief/faith system took over and spoke to them about the possibility of what could be. Potential is all around us waiting to be discovered.

Suspend your disbelief, dare to dream, and become the person you've always wanted to be. Remember, Jesus never prayed the problem. Never stood on unbelief. He called health into beings, life into the dead, and cleansed souls of demons. His thoughts were elevated. Let's elevate ours!

When we change our thoughts, feelings and inner belief system about circumstances and situations, miraculous things are allowed to happen.

I once met a woman who wanted to go under the knife and get a face lift because she thought men found her unattractive, and she also feared that she was shrinking, and that men did not notice her. In her mind, she was the invisible shrinking woman, until I spoke with her and shared my thoughts on reinventing oneself by holding inner dialogues, standing guard over your mind, and screening all negative thoughts.

Once she realized that change is an inside job, she began to emit a radiance which pays homage to every line life's journey has blessed her face with, filling her with compassion as only one who has been there can have. Today her inner beauty shines through and she is the belle of the ball wherever she goes. And she figuratively stands head and shoulders above the crowd.

Let us move on to some thoughts and reflections that will help you get your life in order – in the order that you choose. This time you're in the driver's seat, making conscious decisions, which will produce a happier, more joyful you.

Before we start, close your eyes and see yourself folded into a ball, surrounded by pitch-blackness. Then imagine you are consumed from within by radiant heat, which causes you to pulsate with deep inner joy, an emotion that is beyond words, a feeling that can only be expressed by a sudden explosion of movement, as a budding seedling breaking through hard earth. See yourself as you unfold and rise out of darkness, moving toward and groping for the light, shaking away soil, dirt and dankness; fully grown, filled with fresh hope, dreams, and a radiant newness that glows from inside. With arms thrust toward heaven, you shout "All thanks be to God!"

"Reaching For Freedom"

Reach for freedom by releasing all of the things that anchor and chain you to past moments of regret. Free your bitter memories, give them permission to take flight, then feel and revel in the lightness of being that fills your soul.

"Put Reality on Hold"

If you are widowed and alone don't sit around and mope. Make a date with your best gal pal of thirty years, get dressed to the nines, and head for the most upscale section of town, and go on a shopping spree. Your dearly departed husbands would approve of a little tender loving care. Certainly they would approve of some comfort food; chocolate cake. So why not go wild and pick up that purple Bentley, to match Dora's hair. Not to be out done, give your friend Faye a diamond-studded white gold watch from the high-end celebrity jewelry store of your choice. Check out the upscale restaurants for the evening's bill of fare, pour over the menus without giving the price list a care. Then, together board the bus for home, and laughing stride arm in arm into your favorite neighborhood Deli and order the special of the day. "Happiness is to be lived now. Don't wait until tomorrow. Even if you have to live it out in your most sumptuous dreams."

"Dance Away Your Cares"

Forget all of your woes. Put life's stresses aside. Swing your partner, do-si-do, click your heels, stomp the floor, listen to the caller. Lose yourself in shuffling sawdust, swinging petticoats, and buckskin fringes of rawhide. Let your eyes sparkle, and your cheeks blush red, as you tip your cowboy hat to your lady fair, while watching the wind caresses her hair.

"Reflections"

We have lived long, and hopefully learned much. It is time now to search our minds, hearts and souls for the things that will heal and make us whole. Rediscover the things that you longed to do, or desired to be. Find something that is comparable and do it. If you wanted to be a nun, or do missionary work, find a service organization where you can devote time as a caregiver.

Don't be afraid to dream. You weren't when you were a kid. Unbind your inner child. Release the compassion in your veiled eyes, and the wisdom in your heart. Life is filled with miracles, large and small. But most of us move blindly through the world, missing the possibilities, seeing only an existence colored by the limitations of past conditioning; with downcast eyes we move toward the end. Stop that, now! Take in the beauty of the world God gave, it's free. And, if sight has gone its way, feel natures caress on your skin, breathe in the changing season, baking bread, perfumes, smells of youth, the aged, let them open your mind's eye, to things once seen, or, never seen, but felt with other God given senses.

As a fellow traveler moving along the less traversed road of life, I offer you my hand and bid you accept it, and let your mind take flight. Give yourself permission to soar with me through the cloudy looking glass of life. Behold the dreams beyond dreams, the story behind the story, envision a world of grand possibilities that has always been there, ready and waiting for you, and me, to perceive it. It is time for you to open your heart and allow yourself to appreciate all of the natural wonders that were created and given to you by grace. Enjoy them! Stand in awe of the beauty of a sunset. Give thanks for the dawn of a new day. Marvel at the splendor of the universe and the world around you.

"Touched By Hidden Feelings"

It is time to wake up and dream. Use the spirit filled healing power of your mind. Embrace life. Taste the tears of joy and laughter. Pulsate with vigor. Savor it all, the bitter and the sweet. Experience a moment of laughter, a moment of pain, and then begin again.

And, if you dreamed as a child that there are angels amongst us, dream the dream of angels again and shine from within, as you pay homage to life by dancing freely with the wind. Lift your face into the rain let the wind blow through your hair. Enjoy being a spiritual being having human experiences.

"Reconstructing"

Allow yourself to change from the inside. The new, kinder, gentler you will shine through, because it is all an inside job. The world within will cast its radiant glow on the world without. What we think and feel shapes our external world much more than we care to think. So, once again, I caution you, stand guard over your mind. Be careful of the thoughts you dwell on. They can and do guide and shape our lives. And, after countless hours of entertaining negative or positive thoughts and feelings we make manifest these emotions by words and deeds until they begin to guide and shape our lives.

So if you're used to feeling and thinking, "With my luck, I knew I'd fail," you will set into motion incidents that will indeed fulfill your prophecy of doom. These negative emotions, if dwelled upon long enough, can become tangible physical illnesses, and if held and embraced with great fear, they can cause death.

If you want to manifest thoughts in your life as realities, why not choose to make them uplifting and positive. Try thinking: "I knew things would turn around for the better." "There is always a way to make a win - win situation." Find a way to take adverse circumstances and turn them around. Examine the flip side. Seek out and uncover the values hidden within seemingly bad situations. Focus on short-term goals. When you achieve them build bigger long-term goals. And if the goals fail, profit by the mistakes you have made by analyzing them through the eyes of a confident new you. Write the failures off by realizing what doesn't work, then forge ahead until you find what does work.

"Fear and Doubts"

Often we find it easier to hide our fears and doubts under a veil of silence. But it is not. For in the light of truth the darkest of anxieties and fears fade. When there is clarity and understanding, no Matter how grave the shock, with the facts before us, we can regroup and face the dreaded issue head on.

Granted, when we talk about positive changes, negative thoughts will try and invade our minds and attempt to pull us into a downtrodden state of being. Do not deny their existence. Acknowledge them, diffuse the anger, fear and frustration that are certain to come, and move on. It would be like celebrating the joys of birth, without acknowledging the presence and certainty of death -- to which begins our inevitable journey with our first breath(s).

It has been said throughout the ages that to err is human. Things will inevitably happen to throw us off course, but the secret is to learn the lesson, move on and try not to regress. Don't beat yourself up. Use the experience, reorganize yourself, and grow from the consequences of your actions. Then get back on track.

Remember what threw you off course. Keep a mental or written journal of the old habit patterns that you/we so comfortably slipped back into. This way you/we can spot them in the future and avoid the pitfalls. If not, and you find yourself down in the dumps again briefly wallow in the pain. Prolonged indulgence is not wise. Pity can become a close companion. So, move on quickly.

When going through or while recovering from these dark times, always remember that out of all darkness come rays of light. Light always conquers darkness. Light dissolves the darkest despairs of the heart. You can aid the light to come with a laugh, a smile or a happy little tune born out the sadness of the moment. Laugh through your tears. Reach into that quiet place within and find the rays of hope, which reside inside.

Remember, you are changing from the inside out. You are reinventing yourself one beautiful thought, one wonderful moment, at a time. It is all an inside job. You must always remember that, for it will be a comforting companion on this fascinating journey toward newness, happiness, and involvement with the world of positive change that is waiting for you.

"The True You"

Don't try to compete with youth. You've had your time with the fires and passions of puppy love. Go with what you've got. Respect your wrinkles. This is the second half of your life. Enjoy it! All of it! You've earned that right. The fact is you've run the first half of your marathon, and you are still going, like that little bunny.

Now, it is time to get involved and start enjoying those things you have kept tucked away, secretly hidden in your heart of desires and longings. Do the things you have yearned to do. Do them! Do them if you can. You owe it to yourself. Your winter years can be as barren or as bright as you would have them be. It is all up to you. Don't let life pass you by because of one poor excuse or the other.

Do not attempt to compete with the youth crowd. Enjoy where you are. Enjoy your age. Enjoy who you are. Do not be seduced by breast implant, tummy tucks, more hair, smoother skin and washboard abdominal muscles. Leave the washboard in grandmother's basement beside the homemade ice cream machine and your old Red Flyer snow sled. Sure, keep fit, but don't be seduced by the ad man. Your wrinkles and thinning hair are tributes of valor and are to be worn like battle chevrons, with pride and graciousness. For you have won a war of sorts. Be proud of your thinning hair and that middle-aged spread. Savor yourself like a fine wine that only gets better with the passage of time. In fact, take a picture of yourself, paste it on a bottle of your "private reserve," with a caption, "We get better with age."

People in the "Winter Years" who have not been seduced by the ad man, if asked the question "What would you rather have --love or sex?", would easily answer "love," knowing that it is a package deal. Love with marriage is the given. Sex only adds to the meal. It is not the main course, and as the sands of time fall through the hourglass(s) of our lives, the hot flame of passion flickers, flares brightly and dies out. But, the flame of true love flickers and burns eternal.

Seek true love in all that you do, be it in friendship, work, romance or enjoying the silence. Seek true love in the wind, the sun, the moon, stars and every God given breath you take.

Seek and you too will find the Golden Flower of winter amidst the new fallen snows of winter love, fraught with gratefulness. Let it help light your way on a joyful journey through the rest of your life. Embrace winter love; let it fill your heart anew with a glow that was never there before. Allow it to give you permission to love yourself. Allow it to let you love life and all the amazing things it offers. Allow it to give you eyes of wisdom to perceive the true wonders our Creator brought forth for us to enjoy, and have dominion over.

"The Living God"

God is not removed from you, sitting somewhere in the sky on a cloud. He dwells with you (Emmanuel) and will be in you. Just call Him forth. He is here with us, ready and willing to hear our prayers. So fill yourself with "The Word," and God will communicate with you. And when He does, have a real dialogue with Him. Listen to what He has to say. And, answer Him. Make it a real conversation. He likes that. Not some one-sided monologue. Talk to Him about your needs and the needs of those around you. Then open yourself to His guidance, His will. But, first empower yourself by the authority of the name of Jesus. For as it is written and stated by Jesus, "I am the way, the truth and the life. "No one comes to the Father except through me."

"Take the Time"

Before you rush into prayer, remember, and respect the glory and majesty of who and what God is. Glorify Him. Exalt Him. Praise. Recall all of the things of grace given to you. And, feel the stinging tears of sadness and joy, as you give praise and thanks, for Jesus' sacrifice on the cross. And, as you eat the body and drink the blood, take the time to think. Think what it means to pick up your cross and follow Jesus. Believe your actions will become less focused on this natural world.

There is beauty in all things. But, we must look with the heart to see and truly perceive it.

CELEBRATE LIFE BY SHARING THE BLESSING

Use the following list to jump-start your mind, then pick something enjoyable from your life experiences and share it/them with others.

"The Joy Around Us"

Enjoy your days. God made them, and they are all good. Lift your face to the pouring rain, enjoy the sting of a blustery wind; thrill to the to sight of a sunset; stand in awe of the majesty of the wilderness; feel the hand of God at work when you see a hummingbird in flight, or drink in the beauty of a flower in full bloom. Share these things with a shy friend. It is one of the richest gifts you can give. Or, share a passing thought with a stranger. Then you'll be strangers no more.

"Rich man/Poor man/Beggar man"

I am my brother's keeper, and for that bit of grace I am blessed, for without the bonds of human exchange, we are adrift on a sea of frivolity, in search of meaningless things to pour into our bottomless cups, which we will never get filled up, with the likes of such perishable stuff. Never, no, never drop a bill into a homeless person's cup, or shove it at him/her without connecting with a look, a smile, a touch of human kindness.

"Open the Windows of Your Heart"

If you're feeling lonely and alone, take a trip down memory lane to happier times. Recall milking the cows and observing their contented ways. Embrace gentler times. Enfold that sense of peace; take it into the world and form a circle of joy. Give to the life that has given so much to you. Take advantage of things you know. Become a docent in the museum of natural history; inform small tour groups of grade school children on the evolution of western longhorn cattle. Use what you know to enlighten others. A more informed world will in time make for a more unified world.

"Extend a Helping Hand"

Become a part of "Stephen Ministry." It is a one-to-one ministry by a training, caring friend. Reach out and help those who are experiencing: loneliness, loss of spouse, retirement changes, unemployment, discouragement, childbirth, hospitalization, divorce, grief, terminal illness, being shut-in, questions about God and faith. Become "that" special friend.

"With A Warm Loving Heart"

Welcome them one and all. The old. The new. The happy. The sick. The sad. Make them one and all at home in our house of God. Extend the warmth of a Sunday Southern fried chicken dinner and a little white country church, where there are no strangers, only old friends and new friends to be. Let that be our mentality, be our church large or small.

Join the "Ministry of Ushers." Help your pastor keep his/her growing flock growing. Shepherd them into the fold with everlasting love, care, and compassion.

"Sharing the Gift"

Maybe the trophies are dusty in the display case, and the rail-thin track star in the varsity sweater is only a dim memory behind cloudy eyes that once dreamed of Olympic gold, but if the distant roar of the crowd from days long gone still floods your mind and warms your heart, help others experience the joy of victory, the taste of defeat, and the spirit of trying. Be one of the old jocks that never die.

Become part of the Special Olympics. Be a coach, be a sideline Barnabus, be a sideline supporter, but, be there to urge "that kid" on, with open arms and a willing heart. Let him/ her see you kneeling on the track, with arms spread wide, urging the last runner in the field on to the greatest victory of all; the victory of a spirit that tried. Help a young athlete feel the joy you once felt, straining to extend your personal best. On this day, in the face and eyes of "that child", racing falteringly into your arms, you have arrived. You've bested your personal best. Give back! It is only time, but time that means so much.

"Reaffirming the Joys of Love"

As you move into the sunset of your life, reaffirm your love with a spoken and unspoken tie that binds your hearts and souls, as your physical bodies decline. Let the spirit of holding hands continue to link your lives, like the bridge in the, Japanese Bonsai park, where you pledged to spend your lives together so many winters ago. Pledge, again, to unite your love, forever here on earth, and in the hereafter. May your love endure the changing seasons and grow ever stronger, through rain, sleet and snow. May your love withstand the blistering sun, and weather humbly like the redwood connecting your Bonsai Bridge, and allow your love to stand in tribute, long after you have turned to dust.

"The Beauty Within"

So her hair is thinning and wrinkles fill her face,
and her body is much thicker than before. Does that mean
you cannot be friends anymore? No holding of hands? Or
walks in the park? Do not be hesitant to be seen with her
until it is dark. Her heart is brighter now than when she had
radiant lustrous hair, a body that could compare with a
princess on a golden stair, a porcelain smooth face and a
careless mind with not a serious thought, care or concern.
But, now that she is filled with deep feelings, compassion,
caring and concerns to spare, is it too late for you to be
there?

Answer her with not a word, but let the firm grasp
of your hand holding hers, and the pride in your eyes
express the welling feelings of love you hold inside.

"Elegant Ebony Woman"

Now that her hair is white as snow, standing in
grand tribute above blazing black and ebony skin, with a
few white whiskers on her now withered chin, help her
navigate the steps of the church, and the isle within, clad in
her best Sunday dress, help her into the pew, hold her with
adoring eyes, let your soul reassure her soul, to you, she is

still finer than Sheba, queen of the Nile. Then share that secret smile.

"Be Not the Bearer of Grudges"

If you have offended anyone in any way, knowingly or unknowingly, beg forgiveness for any wrong or hurt that you may have caused him or her. And ask forgiveness for any known or unknown hurt that you may have caused. Then ask forgiveness for any known or unknown hurts or resentments you may hold against them. Humbly ask that you both may be set free of all anger and resentment, and allow the healing to begin and stay the hardening of your hearts. You may never be the best of friends, but never be the bitterest of enemies. And mutually exercise the power of forgiveness, to free yourselves from past anger, hurts, and grievances so dim that memory fails to recall the hurt at all.

"Fifty/Sixty/Seventy Years And Still Going"

Celebrate that landmark day! Give yourself a birthday party and share it with your friends. You can always take that solo cruise another time. Sharing fun times with old friends and relatives are joys to be stored in the heart and remembered for a lifetime. Leave the photo albums and videotapes to the less-than-young at heart.

"Being There"

Sitting in silence with someone you love is often a deeper expression of feeling than words could ever say. So gratefully accept the comforting presence and stillness. Let them wash away the anguish and cares of the day. Just knowing your soul mate is there puts the world at rest. Wordlessly sharing the patter of rain on the windowpane, the warmth of a blazing fire, the music of Mozart, a glass of Port. Being together gives more meaning to life than a volume of words can ever tell.

"Alone, But Not Lonely"

Like, love, and appreciate yourself. You were made special, from a perfect mold. Accept and give fully to friends, acquaintances and that special loved one. You know that you are not short-changing them on the gift. And, when you are alone treat yourself with the gift and the pleasure of your own company. It teaches you resourcefulness and independence. Often, in solitude we gain greater appreciation of the so-called simple things in life, which are so often very wonderful in, and of themselves.

Dress in your Sunday best. Buy an expensive bottle of wine, remove the label and replace it with a picture of that romantic little retreat in Milan, Italy, and caption it, "Fond Memories."

Enjoy a candlelight dinner alone. Savor your food. Become one with your palate and the beverage of choice. Absorb the fervor of a football crowd. Revel in the chill of the wind, the smell of hot dogs, onions and beer. Keep quality and character in your life at all times. They make the best of friends and companions, for they are oftentimes reminders of how we should treat others, for they signal how wonderful we feel when we are the recipients of thoughtful regard. In other words, "Do unto others."

"Minister to the Needy"

As set forth in Scripture, believers are to witness and serve after the example of Jesus Christ. Minister to those who are in need: to the sick, to the friendless, and any who may be in distress, both within and beyond the community of faith. Be a demonstration of the Christian gospel, both within the church community and in the world. Share gifts of leadership, put your skills to work, become part of a mission that will have far reaching consequences. Volunteer to help plant wells in the Sudan.

"A Prayer of Thanksgiving"

As dusk descends and this day draws to a close, I thank You my Lord and Savior, for seeing me through another day, keeping me safe while on the road, and in the comfort and safety of my home, surrounded by warmth and loved ones. No Matter how grand or small my dwelling may be, the power of this humble prayer spills forth from me. It is offered up with all the passion of a grateful soul, filled with all the praises and wonders that my heart holds.

Praise be to our Creator, for all of the signs and wonders seen through these long living eyes, the mirrors of my vintage soul. Thank you, Heavenly Father, for allowing me to witness the beauty of the many small miracles, which unfold around me in the course of a day. Now, dear Lord, I fold my hands in prayer for this has been another in a series of blessed days.

"Where the Heart Is"

When love abounds, a house becomes a home. Give a lasting gift with the sweat of your brow and help build a home. Christen it with calloused hands, banged-up fingers and an aching back. Take on the venture with a caring heart. Join in with friends. Drive a nail of permanence in the foundation for a house that will possibly become the first home for a deserving family. Keep the circle of love growing; give a family a chance to move into the mainstream of life. With peace and many blessings, may a new family's life begin.

"Celebrate Life by Giving"

Don't ask what you can gain from life; ask what you can give to life. And, don't wait for life to answer back. Get busy giving. There are lots of ways to do it.

"True Joy Is Sharing"

"Dear Lord, it seems that the more I live for myself, the less my life seems to mean. When I seek to please myself, there is no one with whom to share the joy. Please give me a chance to live for others." – Anon

"Clown for a Day"

In the past you might have been Queen or King for a Day and won prizes and cash on a game show. Now, I want you to leave memory lane behind, step into the present time. Slip into the costume of a clown, put on your silliest face and make your way to a children's hospital, or a convalescent home for the elderly. Surround yourself with people who need more love than care; because medical staff and crew provide care. The bushels of love must come from you. Paint their faces, and make them laugh by pulling tiny stuffed animals from the many pockets in your clown suit, and juggle them in the air, then leave your new friends laughing as if they had not a worry or a care.

"Unfulfilled Dreams"

Find a place where you can use your gifts in service to the Lord. Offer and do volunteer work at a mission, a shelter or a halfway house. Work the soup line. Lend an ear to a battered woman. Be a friend to someone who is lonely. Mentor a child in need. Offer a lifeline to someone who is discouraged. Be someone who cares.

"Now I Lay Me Down To Sleep"

Switch out the light and heave a sigh of relief. Put all cares aside and lay down to rest, prayerfully, knowing and saying to God, today I did my level best. Now, leave it all up to Him, knowing that He will best your immeasurable best. And, since you have learned that your best and His best are often light years apart, sit and wait in awesome wonder. Having come to revere the working of His ways, lay all of your cares and plans at the foot of His cross, and pray that you will understand the signs and wonders presented to you. So, nestle your head within the folds of your pillow, and bid sleep come, knowing that His Divine will, will be done.

"Another Day"

Thank You, precious Lord for keeping us through this night. Thank You for the breath of life. Thank You for another day-to try and get it right. Thank You for allowing us to enjoy Your greatest of creations – life.

SECTION FOUR

PERSONAL AND WORLD PRAYERS FOR
INDIVIDUALS AND UNIVERSAL HEALING

"Abandonment"

Please Lord, save me from the cruel coldness I feel that is turning me into a hostile belligerent person. Help me shed all bitter thoughts of the abandonment that all but shattered my life. Let right action set me on a new course. Release my spirit to soar free and clear, into the warmth and beauty of a new life where honor and devotion are held dear. Take me to a place where true friends stand united. No Matter the adversity. Help me rise from the ashes of my shattered dreams, help me find the courage to stop the self abuse, give me courage and strength, to get away from the beatings, then tears, then gifts, and words of forgiveness, and the terror of when it will happen again.

Give me strength to abandon this cycle of insanity.

"Vision Prayer, For a Lost Sheep"

Heavenly Father, blessed Emmanuel, living God among us, we come to you in the name of your son, Jesus Christ, and by His authority, we lay this prayer at the foot of the old rugged cross, knowing you are with us, because of the promise, "Where two or more are gathered". Thus we offer up this prayer. "As You will and as You know, help our beloved, and lost, sister_____, as she is going through this "Dark night of the soul." Lord, lead her through this temporary folly of wild living, and protect her from all harm, by covering her with the powerful blood of Jesus. And, like The Prodigal Son, bring her back to her senses, and return her to the fold, unharmed; wiser, and filled with compassion, and contrition.

In Jesus' name this we pray.

Amen.

"Alcoholism and Substance Abuse"

The mistakes of my past are behind me. The hurts, the pain and the ugliness of long ago I throw out with the garbage and other trash. Now I trust in the word of God to fill my heart, body, mind and soul. No more is healing power found in my favorite stash or my drink of choice.

Forever, dear Lord God, let the waters that quicken my soul flow through me like a babbling brook, keeping me fresh, clean and clear. In Jesus' name this I pray and give thanks for lending me an ear.

"Anger"

Help me control the anger from my past that clouds and distorts my actions at every turn. Give me clarity of mind to take life as it comes. Grant me the strength to fight my abusive past, which causes me to lash out in hurtful ways. Help me stop blaming others as a way of protecting myself. Relieve me of these feelings of persecution that keep my anger at the boiling point, just beneath the surface of my skin. Let me see clearly when the darkness of my childhood colors my visions of the here and now. Help me stop testing and pushing people away with caustic biting words designed to protect me from imagined things that would threaten and hurt my fragile soul, if they were real. I know it is wrong to always want to be right. Please stop me from distorting facts to support my point of view.

Bless me with the peace of knowing that the world is not out to get me. This I pray to God.

"Betrayal"

Free me from the bondage of this damning anger that I hold inside. This sense of utter disloyalty and betrayal rages within clouding everything I see. Cleanse my heart from the bitterness I hold. Help me realize that it is always fear that makes me lash out bitterly, ever cautious of new betrayals that might penetrate my heart.

Grant me the courage to trust again. Let me go forward bathed in Your light, with arms spread wide, ready to welcome and trust what life holds.

"Choices"

Abba Father, bestow upon me a discerning heart, this I pray, as I go through this day. Grant me the wisdom to seek Your counsel for the smallest choice to the largest decision I make during the course of the day. Give me the wisdom to hear the Good Shepherd's voice, and not the voice of a stranger, who would guide me to hidden agendas that would increase profit in a less-than honorable way. Let me act responsibly, for every choice I make has far-reaching consequences. I am everywhere my thoughts and energy flow. Dear Lord, guide my choices from on high. Use me to further Your Kingdom, even though it may be in the smallest way.

"Disabled"

Lord, please don't let the world brand me as disabled, or handicapped, impaired, crippled, unfit, or unqualified. To a stranger I may appear to be less than a whole guy/girl but once he or she gets to know me, their views will surely change.

Lord, let the world see me as you do, just another working stiff, a guy/girl happily driving his car. A weekend jock, a racquetball champion on the outdoor concrete courts. My wheelchair and faith in You give me a supreme advantage against any opponent and obstacle in life. For I am fueled and super charged with Your power inside to accomplish the things You want for me. In Jesus' name this I pray and give thanks.

"Do Not Stand at My Grave and Weep"
Do not stand at my grave and weep
I am not there. I do not sleep.
I am a thousand winds that blow
I am the diamond glints on the snow.
I am the sunlight on ripened grain;
I am the gentle autumn's rain.
When you awaken in the morning's hush,
I am the swift uplifting rush
Of quiet birds in circled flight.
I am the soft star that shines at night.
Do not stand at my grave and cry.
I am not there; I did not die.

Author unknown.

"Empty the Vessel"

Heavenly Father, this I do pray, in the name of Jesus Christ. Grant me the spiritual strength to meet the challenge to empty out my old life and ways so that I may be made full, and new. Give me courage to die to my past and be reborn with redemption and salvation as You guide me along a path of stronger, social attitudes and religious values.

"Fear of Success"

I say I want to succeed, but with thoughts of success I can hardly breathe. Why do I procrastinate and do things to sabotage myself? I make excuses by the score, fearful to seek, ask, find, and knock on the "narrow door" of success.

I dare not speak these things aloud. I am content to complain and make false starts, for I dare not venture forward to find out the truth. Am I good enough?

Heavenly Father, I come to You in the name of Jesus and kneel at the foot of Your cross, heavy laden. Lord give me the power to release past fears. Strengthen me to accept "Thy will," and allow me to receive and accept Your vision of success for me. I lift this up in divine faith that Your will, will be performed, perhaps not as I pray it, but as it should be. Amen.

"Financial Loss"

Free me from the superficial fears that rule my life. Often I used to hide behind money, high-end cars, and a nice house. Empty inside, I was afraid, with no place to escape. Every moment awake or asleep, I feared the loss of my ability to compete honestly. Quite often this fear tempted me to lie and cheat. In the world of business lying and cheating is the norm. It's expected!

Then with a move so blinding swift and neat you took it all. I was pinned to the wall, my empire rubble at my feet. No more the Big Fish in the little pond.

You showed me the way and brought me back with visions of what is true and meaningful in life.

Now through it all I am able to stand tall, surrounded by the riches I'll always keep, no Matter how often I may fall. The love of family and friends is with me as I weather this tide.

With their love and Your blessings Lord, I will more than survive. My true wealth is the quality of love I'm willing to give and receive.

"Freedom to Succeed"

Lonely and alone, I come to you Holy Spirit filled with silent prayers. Free me from the chains that strangle and bind my consciousness. For in the silence of my soul many fears reside. Secrets hidden in dark places control me, keeping me shackled, grasping for a career and self-esteem that seems so near, but yet so out of reach of my grasping fingertips.

Holy Spirit please bring these fears into the light so they will wilt and fade away. Show me that these demons are nothing trying to be something. Clear away the dark shadows in my mind. Free me! Let me walk in my creator's guiding and healing light, along a path that is straight, sure and clear.

Lead me to success in my chosen career. I have prayed and searched my heart, always asking that, "Thy will be done." At those times I'm filled with a supernatural fire, allowing my beliefs to soar higher and higher. So, I believe I'm not being willful, a take-charge person. For I have prayed and searched my heart, looking for signs and wonders that this is truly Your will for me. In my heart of hearts I know these feelings can't be wrong. For You have laid these desires upon my heart.

Give me the strength to be Your instrument in human form. Allow me to hear and follow the Holy Spirit as I am lead through this "Dark Night of the Soul." I humbly thank You my indwelling friend for keeping me from sinking into the pit of despair. I praise You for the many times You've lifted me up, as I kept trying to do it my way. Willfully! On my own! Without prayer! I was stuck in a gigantic rut for many a year.

Now I praise and thank the Holy Spirit for freeing my mind of those needless fears and showing me what to say and do so I can play the melodies and perform in a fashion to glorify and edify You Lord. Now I walk by faith and not by what is seen. I follow the voice of the Good Shepherd like a wilderness guide leading me through the dense darkness, bringing me safely into the light. And standing in that powerful healing light, I know that I will accomplish all of the things, You, my Heavenly Father has laid upon my heart. In Jesus' name this I pray and give thanks to You.

"Grief"

Precious Jesus, grant me the strength not to grieve, wail and mourn. For You have given us seasons for all things. The countdown to the season of death begins with our first breath.

So my friend, I will not grieve your passing, for it would put a pall over a life, which was so well spent, a life full to overflowing with the joys of giving, and shared friendships and laughter. I will not mourn you by wearing designer basic black, knowing your penchant for fashion. In selfish ways I will deeply regret the physical loss. Not seeing your smiling face, enjoying the warmth of your presence, and the clothes you so carefully chose to wear to highlight your angel face. But, I as well as all who knew you will see the vibrancy of your being and hear the resounding words of encouragement and confidence you exchanged with us one and all. Private, precious moments shared in trust will forever resound in our hearts, and through our mind's eye will see you with vision so clear.

And, as long as memory lives you will never die. Live happy, up there, in one of His many mansions. We'll see you when it's time.

"Harmony"

Precious Lord, I kneel before you in reverent prayer. Please give me a place where I can feel safe and call home, a space where I can maintain my principles, dignity and faith without damaging my spirit and energy. Surround me with positive forces, people, objects, books, things that uplift and edify. Permit me to move in circles of respect, harmony and joy. Fill every area of my life to overflowing with mental, emotional, physical, and spiritual well-being. Bathe me in Your guiding light, that I may live a pure life and do what is right in Your sight. But, until you grant this prayer, I thank you for this car, which keeps from the shelter of doorways.

"He Heals Me From Within"

I banish all fears of growths, lumps and diseases that are legacies from my family's past. I claim and receive healing. I am healed, whole and new. Thank You, Heavenly Father, for blessing me with the power of prayer. In Jesus' mighty name I give thanks.

"Infertile"

With hands clasped in prayer and tears streaming from my eyes, Heavenly Father, this I pray, make my body fertile. Please drive the barrenness away. Allow my womb to grow and swell with the magic of life. Allow me to give my husband the joy he's so long been waiting to hear the sound of little ones transforming our house into a home.

"Infertility"

Heavenly Father, we united in holy matrimony to be as one. And it was a most joyous day filled with love, harmony and bliss, sharing many a marital kiss. The many years since have been filled with blessings. But, we still long for that blessed event. You know our hearts, Lord, and our desire for a child/children. So, I/we kneel beneath Your holy cross praying that You will make our bonding complete by allowing us to have a baby girl or a bouncing baby boy. Please let us have a child of our own.

"Isolation"

Lord, liberate me from this isolation, which haunts me day and night. Release me from feeling that I am always a shadow in the crowd, still my pounding heart. Stop the pulsating doubt that strangles the speech in my throat. Give me the courage to let others near, still the nervousness within me that causes me to run away. Let me accept a kind word, a casual smile and take the offered hand of friendship, without slipping into my shell.

"Issues of Health"

I accept no disease or condition that attempts to make me terminally ill. I invoke the healing power of Jesus that resides within me to combat this condition which medical science has given a name. I put myself in the hands of doctors and their capable staff. But, reverently I call upon the power of Jesus to guide and direct the doctors and caregivers as they minister to me. And, when all is said and done they will marvel at the medical miracle before them. But, in my heart of hearts I will know it was my Heavenly Father's work. The greatest surgeon of All!

"Love's Power"

Imbue me with the power to love, to be compassionate, to dedicate myself to causes of right action. Help me inspire others. Help me give hope and instill trust in others as well as myself. Give me the ability to infuse others with a radiant kindness, which flows from my heart, a kindness which speaks louder than shouted words.

"Making a Living"

Can I make a living through these waning years? The job market is shrinking with every coming day. I am older now and looked upon by many as past my prime. But I have experience, and then some, to spare. And I'm filled with an honest work ethic and good cheer. So, dear Lord, let not your handiwork be discarded before my work is done upon this earthly plane. Please, let me use the gifts You so richly blessed me with. Let me share them with the world at large.

I never want to be the boss. I know who is in charge. So, I sit by the telephone, asking for Thy will to be done in my life.

"Need of Employment"

Thank You Heavenly Father for a job that will allow me to provide the basic necessities of life for my family and me. Thank You giving me an opportunity to live once again with human dignity. Thank You God for providing a means for me to put a roof over our heads that we can call home. This I pray and give thanks, in the name of Jesus.

"Not a Burden, But a Joy"

Let me not be a great source of worry or stress. Let me not become someone that is emotionally difficult to abide. Let me not become a duty or responsibility that is a source of vexation, worry or hardship. Let me not become a millstone around the necks of those I love. Let me be someone to share a laugh with, a hug or even a tear. Dear Lord, let my family and friends accept the storehouse of prayers, blessings and good wishes I hold for them one and all, until the end of my days. In Jesus' name this I pray.

"Partner of My Own"

You above all know that we are not meant to be alone. You paired the creatures that boarded the ark two-by-two. I miss the oneness of being us. You know I'm not perfect by any means. So, Dear Lord, bring me someone imperfect like me, so that we can get on with the business of being we, instead of just me.

"Self-pity"

Why am I always wrong? Why are they always right? Why am I always out of step? Why are they looking at me that way? Is it my Thrift Shop clothes? Not everybody wastes money they don't have on designer labels. I know those furtive glances; the whispering and the nasty giggles are about me. I can feel their criticism soiling my soul. Why am I always getting stabbed in the back? Why am I last on every list? Why do all of the phony popular people get the things I want?

...Why am I never invited to social events? Is it because I'm too fat, too thin, or too short? Too tall, too Black, too Blonde, too ginger? Why doesn't anybody ever call? When they do invite me out I know it's to pick on me and show me up.

They always flaunt their new cars, clothes and things. Usually they are gifts from lovers, family and friends. Nobody gives me anything. Not even the time of day, on a broken watch. And when I receive a gift, a smile or a touch I see the disingenuousness in their eyes.

Oh, God! Help me close the gate and leave this pity party behind. Give me the courage not to look back at the failures I have made, the nagging irritations that I allow to fester and create nasty things in my mind.

Help me step into Your blessed white light that will wash away all of my feelings of self-pity, failure and regret. Let me recognize the beauty in my life and come to a place of healing and self-acceptance.

"Universal Healing Prayer, Time for Healing"

Heavenly Father, help me look beyond the terrorism and devastation that is happening globally. Give me the strength to look beyond that, which is seen. Allow me to envision that which is unseen; peace and unity.

Help me feel the beauty of Your Divine Plan. Lift my heart, strengthen my faith, and help me trust, in Your design for a greater, more unified and spiritual world. I pray for a coming together of religions, nations, commonwealths and countries, as never before, and will stand united for human rights.

With this coming together I pray for a world of peace and goodwill amongst all people and religions. May the people who are righteous in heart stand and endure forever and ever more.

Help me see beyond the man-made chaos and confusion that we created out of blind hatred.

Allow me the perseverance to withstand these uncertain times. Fortify my faith as I lift up this state of global unrest with prayers for peace, healing, rebirth and the unification of all nations in loving peace.

"Wisdom"

Father, grant me wisdom, knowledge and understanding daily. Help me remember "That You are the truth, the way, and the life." And, in this wisdom, plant my feet firmly upon Your path and let me not waver during the course of this day. Allow me to rest, assured in the knowledge that I am in You and You are in me.

<u>"Unification of Churches"</u>

Oh, Lord, what a glorious day it will be when people of all faiths, creeds, colors and countries, representing every Heritage and culture, come together as one in Your house. I lift this desire up to You in Your son's precious and holy name. In Jesus' name this I pray. Amen.

IN PARTING

Remember, Prayer is the power beyond belief. If you believe that your glass is half empty, who am I to dispute that? But, let me share a thought with you. If your half-empty glass is filled with remorse and bitter regret, empty it out. And, prayerfully refill your glass to half full with things you like. Then make your life good to the last drop. Remember you have prayer at your disposal; the Power that is beyond belief.

ABOUT THE AUTHOR

I was the youngest of five siblings, born in Michigan and raised in California. I began writing at an early age, because being a small child, it allowed me to dream big and create worlds where I was "the savior" and not the victim.

After many trying years growing up in a very tough neighborhood, a stint in the armed forces expanded my world view, and I stumbled into the world of screen writing, and realized why I had been spared the fate of many of my peers, who died in the streets of South Central Los Angeles, or wound up in prison.

God had, and has, a purpose for my life, to write things to help inspire and uplift the human condition; which is not exactly what I was doing as a screen and television writer. On a few occasions I wrote things I was actually not ashamed of, as I look back.

My turning point came in the late 80's and early 90's when I found myself a divorced, single parent, with an 8 year-old- son. Life was coming at me, with a tidal wave of things that I couldn't handle, so I did what I saw my mother (who virtually raised our family alone) do, I found a church where my son would find Jesus, accept God and find the things he needed.

Little did I know, that it was I who was in need and in great peril, I was using the gift of writing that I was given by grace, to turn out product that was less than grace filled.

Upon my epiphany I wrote a screenplay that won a Christopher Award, a high honor for bringing quality work to the small screen. After that, I realized that I was a child of the most high God, saved by grace and the blood of Jesus. Since that time I have become involved actively with my church, as a deacon, an usher, a Communion server, a prayer team member and a called minister (Lay Minister) who shares faith and life experiences with at-risk youth. And, in 2011 I was the keynote speaker for the Fellowship of Christian Athletes. On occasion, I still write for film and television, but I choose projects that will inspire hope, faith and belief in God.

I pick film projects that speak to life's trial and triumphs through faith, because --- In a journey filled with challenges; highs and lows, ups and downs, I have learned that the only support system which has never failed me, is God, Jesus Christ, the Holy Spirit--- and the Bible, God's written word. To me, it is the answer book, for all of life's question; large or flyspeck small.

TO ILLUSTRATE THE POWER OF PRAYER

Scripture says "If ye have faith as a grain of mustard seed, ye shall say unto this mountain, Remove hence to yonder place; and it shall move; and nothing shall be impossible unto you." Mark 11:23 says, "For verily I say unto this mountain, Be thou removed, and be thou cast into the sea: and shall not doubt in his heart, but shall believe that those things which he saith shall come to pass; he shall have whatsoever he saith."

MY STORY

A rich man moved next door to my home and built a two story house which invaded the privacy of my yard, then planted a fence line of 10 to 11 foot bamboo stalks to ensure his privacy. I prayed for money to do the same on my property, ignoring a small weed 2 feet tall growing beside my fence. God did not bring the money I prayed for to buy bamboo, but He allowed that weed to flourish into a full blown tree, fifty feet tall, that towers above my neighbors house; giving me privacy as well.

"God always answers prayer (s) , not always in the way we
request, but always, with what is best."

"You will seek me and find me when you seek me with all your heart." Jeremiah 29:13

Let us pray.

Author, Charles Johnson

Made in the USA
San Bernardino, CA
23 February 2020

64864882R00122